ENGLISH

3A

in Common

Student Book/Workbook
with ActiveBook

Richard Acklam   Araminta Crace

Series Consultants
María Victoria Saumell and Sarah Louisa Birchley

ALWAYS LEARNING

PEARSON

English in Common 3A
Student Book/Workbook Split Edition

Pearson Education, 10 Bank Street, White Plains, NY 10606

Staff credits: The editorial, design, production, and manufacturing people who make up the *English in Common 3* team are Margaret Antonini, Allen Ascher, Rhea Banker, Eleanor Kirby Barnes, Mike Boyle, Tracey Cataldo, Aerin Csigay, Mindy DePalma, Dave Dickey, Chris Edmonds, Mike Kemper, Jessica Miller-Smith, Laurie Neaman, Loretta Steeves, and Charlie Green.

This series is dedicated to Charlie Green. Without Charlie's knowledge of pedagogy, strong work ethic, sense of humor, patience, perseverance, and creativity, *English in Common* would never have existed.

Cover design: Tracey Cataldo
Cover photo: © qushe/shutterstock.com
Text design: Tracey Cataldo
Text composition: TSI Graphics
Text font: MetaPlus

ISBN 13: 978-0-13-262875-4
ISBN 10: 0-13-262875-9

Library of Congress Cataloging-in-Publication Data
Bygrave, Jonathan
    English in common. Book 1 / Jonathan Bygrave.
        p. cm.
    ISBN 0-13-247003-9—ISBN 0-13-262725-6—
ISBN 0-13-262727-2—ISBN 0-13-262728-0—
ISBN 0-13-262729-9—ISBN 0-13-262731-0
1. English language—Textbooks for foreign speakers.
2. English language—Grammar.
3. English language—Spoken English.
    PE1128.B865 2011
    428.24--dc23

2011024736

Photo Credits: All photos are used under license from Shutterstock.com except for the following. Page 7 (bottom right) iStockphoto.com; p. 12 (middle top) Photolibrary.com, (middle bottom) Christie's Images/Corbis, (right top) Hulton Archive/Getty Images, (right bottom) UPPA/Photoshot/Newscom; p. 17 (D) Dreamstime.com; p. 18 RD/Kirkland/Retna Ltd./Corbis; p. 22 (left) AP Images/Dan Steinberg, (middle) AP Images/Evan Agostini; p. 28 AP Images/Johnny Green; p. 30 (bottom) Foodcollection.com/Alamy; p. 35 Fotolia.com; p. 38 (top) Royal Geographical Society /Alamy, (bottom) Buzz Pictures/Alamy; p. 55 (left) AP Images/Matt Sayles, (middle) AF archive/Alamy, (right) Twentieth Century Fox/Photofest; p. 59 (left) Moviestore Collection Ltd/Alamy; p. 60 Bettmann/Corbis; p. 62 PA Photos; Workbook Page 5 Stockbyte; Workbook p. 7 (top left) Shutterstock.com, (right) Shutterstock.com, (bottom left) iStockphoto.com; Workbook p. 10 Glen A. Baker/Redferns Music Picture Library; Workbook p. 11 Shutterstock.com; Workbook p. 13 Shutterstock.com; Workbook p. 14 Shutterstock.com; Workbook p. 15 Press Association Images; Workbook p. 32 (left) Mary Evans Picture Library, (right) Frank Sutton/Rex Features; Workbook p. 34 Parrot Pascal/Corbis SYGMA; Workbook p. 37 (top) Shutterstock.com, (bottom) Shutterstock.com; Workbook p. 39 Jenny Acheson/Axiom Photographic Agency Ltd.

Illustration Credits: Student Book illustrated by: Judy Brown, Noel Ford, Stephane Gamain (nb illustration), Neil Gower, Alex Green (Folio), Dominic li (The Organisation), Sally Newton, Andrew Pavitt (The Organisation), Roger Penwill and Lucy Truman (New Division). Workbook illustrated by: Mike Phillips, Theresa Tibbetts, Colin Brown, Martin Sanders, Jon Mitchell, Janos Jantner, Phil Garner (all from Beehive Illustrations).

Printed in the United States of America
1 2 3 4 5 6 7 8 9 10—V082—16 15 14 13 12

Contents

English in Common 3
with ActiveBook

Maria Victoria Saumell
Sarah Louisa Birchley

PEARSON

English in Common is a six-level course that helps adult and young-adult English learners develop effective communication skills that correspond to the Common European Framework of Reference for Languages (CEFR). Every level of *English in Common* is correlated to a level of the CEFR, and each lesson is formulated around a specific CAN DO objective.

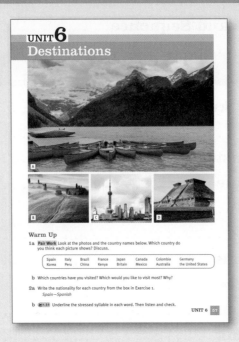

UNIT 6
Destinations

Warm Up

1a **Pair Work** Look at the photos and the country names below. Which country do you think each picture shows? Discuss.

| Spain | Italy | Brazil | France | Japan | Canada | Colombia | Germany |
| Korea | Peru | China | Kenya | Britain | Mexico | Australia | the United States |

b Which countries have you visited? Which would you like to visit most? Why?

2a Write the nationality for each country from the box in Exercise 1.
Spain—Spanish

b Underline the stressed syllable in each word. Then listen and check.

UNIT 6 57

English in Common 3 has twelve units. Each unit has ten pages.

There are three two-page lessons in each unit.

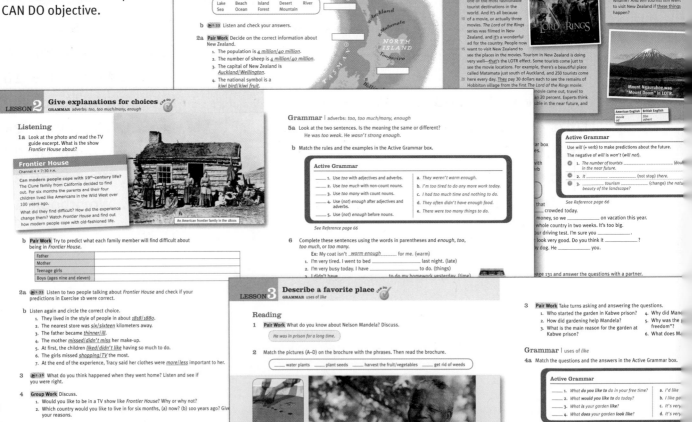

LESSON 1 Make general predictions about the future CAN DO
GRAMMAR will: predictions

Listening

1a **Pair Work** Complete the map (1–7) with the words in the box. Which words **can't** you use?

| Lake | Beach | Island | Desert | River |
| Sea | Ocean | Forest | Mountain | |

b Listen and check your answers.

2a **Pair Work** Decide on the correct information about New Zealand.
1. The population is 4 million/40 million.
2. The number of sheep is 4 million/40 million.
3. The capital of New Zealand is Auckland/Wellington.
4. The national symbol is a kiwi bird/kiwi fruit.

LESSON 2 Give explanations for choices CAN DO
GRAMMAR adverbs: too, too much/many, enough

Listening

1a Look at the photo and read the TV guide excerpt. What is the show *Frontier House* about?

Frontier House
Channel 4 • 7:30 P.M.

Can modern people cope with 19th-century life? The Clune family from California decided to find out. For six months the parents and their four children lived like Americans in the Wild West over 100 years ago.

What did they find difficult? How did the experience change them? Watch *Frontier House* and find out how modern people cope with old-fashioned life.

An American frontier family in the 1800s

b **Pair Work** Try to predict what each family member will find difficult about being in *Frontier House.*

Father	
Mother	
Teenage girls	
Boys (ages nine and eleven)	

2a Listen to two people talking about *Frontier House* and check if your predictions in Exercise 1b were correct.

b Listen again and circle the correct choice.
1. They lived in the style of people in about 1818/1880.
2. The nearest store was six/sixteen kilometers away.
3. The father became thinner/ill.
4. The mother missed/didn't miss her make-up.
5. At first, the children liked/didn't like having so much to do.
6. The girls missed shopping/TV the most.
7. At the end of the experience, Tracy said her clothes were more/less important to her.

3 What do you think happened when they went home? Listen and see if you were right.

4 **Group Work** Discuss.
1. Would you like to be in a TV show like *Frontier House*? Why or why not?
2. Which country would you like to live in for six months, (a) now? (b) 100 years ago? Give your reasons.

60

Grammar | adverbs: too, too much/many, enough

5a Look at the two sentences. Is the meaning the same or different?
He was too weak. He wasn't strong enough.

b Match the rules and the examples in the Active Grammar box.

Active Grammar

___ 1. Use too with adjectives and adverbs.	a. They weren't warm enough.
___ 2. Use too much with non-count nouns.	b. I'm too tired to do any more work today.
___ 3. Use too many with count nouns.	c. I had too much time and nothing to do.
___ 4. Use (not) enough after adjectives and adverbs.	d. They often didn't have enough food.
___ 5. Use (not) enough before nouns.	e. There were too many things to do.

See Reference page 66

6 Complete these sentences using the words in parentheses and enough, too, too much, or too many.
Ex: My coat isn't warm enough for me. (warm)
1. I'm very tired. I went to bed ___ last night. (late)
2. I'm very busy today. I have ___ to do. (things)
3. I didn't have ___ to do my homework yesterday. (time)

LESSON 3 Describe a favorite place CAN DO
GRAMMAR uses of like

Reading

1 **Pair Work** What do you know about Nelson Mandela? Discuss.
He was in prison for a long time.

2 Match the pictures (A–D) on the brochure with the phrases. Then read the brochure.

___ water plants   ___ plant seeds   ___ harvest the fruit/vegetables   ___ get rid of weeds

Garden of Freedom

The charity *Seeds for Africa* has started its first prison vegetable garden in Kabwe Prison in Zambia. There are 500 prisoners at Kabwe Prison, and the prison garden will give them fresh vegetables to eat. More importantly, the prison staff hope that the garden will increase the prisoners' self-esteem.

"A garden was one of the few things in prison that I could control. It gave me the simple but important satisfaction of planting a seed, watching it grow, watering it, and then harvesting it. It was a small taste of freedom. In some ways, I saw the garden as being like my life. A leader must also look after his garden; he, too, plants seeds and then watches

3 **Pair Work** Take turns asking and answering the questions.
1. Who started the garden in Kabwe prison?
2. How did gardening help Mandela?
3. What is the main reason for the garden at Kabwe prison?
4. Why did Mand...
5. Why was the p... freedom"?
6. What does Ma...

Grammar | uses of like

4a Match the questions and the answers in the Active Grammar box.

Active Grammar

___ 1. What do you like to do in your free time?	a. I'd like...
___ 2. What would you like to do today?	b. I like ga...
___ 3. What is your garden like?	c. It's very...
___ 4. What does your garden look like?	d. It's very...

See Reference page 66

b Match the definitions with the different uses of like.
___ 1. want or want to do   a. be like
___ 2. enjoy   b. like
___ 3. appearance   c. look like
___ 4. character or characteristics   d. would like

Pronunciation | reductions

5 Listen to sentences 1–2 in the Active Grammar box. How a... you and would you pronounced?

6 **Pair Work** Write questions using like, look like, would like to, or b... ask and answer the questions.
Ex: Do you enjoy gardening?   Do you like gardening?
1. Tell me about your best friend.

iv

A two-page Unit Wrap Up and a Reference page end each unit.

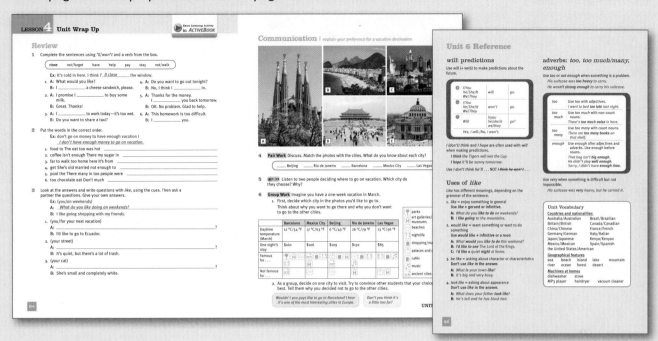

Back of Student Book

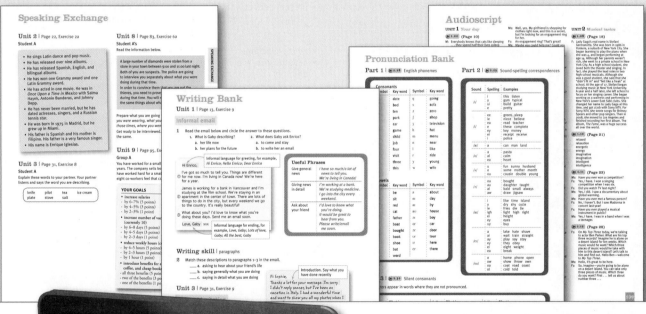

- Each Student Book contains an ***ActiveBook***, which provides the Student Book in digital format. *ActiveBook* also includes the complete Audio Program and Extra Listening activities.

- An optional **MyLab** provides students with the opportunity for extra practice anytime, anywhere.

- The Teacher's Resource Book contains teaching notes, photocopiable extension activities, and an ***ActiveTeach***, which provides a digital Student Book enhanced by interactive whiteboard software. *ActiveTeach* also includes the videos and video activities, as well as the complete Test Bank.

	UNIT	CAN DO OBJECTIVES	GRAMMAR	VOCABULARY/ EXPRESSIONS	
1	**Your day** 3A page 7	• talk about personal likes and dislikes • ask and answer questions about daily routines • write an email to update someone about your life	• likes and dislikes • simple present • adverbs of frequency • present continuous	• verb-noun phrases about routine actions • sleeping habits • stores and shopping • talking about learning needs and abilities	
2	**Musical tastes** 3A page 17	• talk about events in the past • compare yourself to another person • talk about personal achievements and experiences	• simple past • agreement: *so* and *neither* • present perfect and simple past	• music • talking about life events • word families: nouns and adjectives • achievements: collocations • referring to times in the past	
3	**Fine cuisine** 3A page 27	• tell a friend about your future plans • write an informal invitation • make plans with a friend	• *be going to*: future plans • relative clauses (defining) • definite plans: present continuous	• food and restaurants • sensory adjectives and verbs • talking about future plans • describing something you don't know the name of	
4	**Survival** 3A page 37	• compare people • write a thank-you note • ask polite questions	• comparatives • superlatives • indirect questions	• describing people • survival skills • asking questions politely	
5	**Life events** 3A page 47	• exchange opinions with a friend • write a personal profile • describe yourself when you were younger	• modals of obligation: *should, can, have to* • present perfect with *for* and *since* • past routines: *used to*	• life activities • friendship • habits • exchanging opinions with a friend	
6	**Destinations** 3A page 57	• make general predictions about the future • give explanations for choices • describe a favorite place	• *will*: predictions • adverbs: *too, too much/many, enough* • uses of *like*	• geographical features • machines at home • describing natural places • talking about choices	
7	**Mind and body** 3B page 67	• describe a person's physical appearance • describe someone's personality • talk about illness and give advice	• real conditional • gerunds and infinitives • reasons/purpose: *because/ so that/in order to*	• appearance • personality • illness and injury • modifying adjectives • responding to jokes	
8	**Life in the fast lane** 3B page 77	• describe simple changes • find out personal information • ask and answer questions about past actions	• passive voice: present • review of question types • past continuous and simple past	• verbs about change • phrasal verbs—relationships • talking about simple changes	
9	**Careers** 3B page 87	• respond to simple job interview questions • talk about your abilities • write a short article	• *can, could, be able to*: ability • passive voice: past	• work • crime • telling a story	
10	**Animal planet** 3B page 97	• talk about people who influenced you • write a short comment on a blog • speculate about sounds and pictures	• nouns: count/noncount • articles: *the*	• phrasal verbs • animals and zoos • verbs + prepositions • using conversational phrases • speculating	
11	**World travel** 3B page 107	• find out if someone would be a good travel companion • make generalizations about customs • write about a place you've traveled to	• present perfect with *just, yet*, and *already* • verbs with direct and indirect objects • past perfect	• vacation activities • greetings and leave taking • talking about a vacation you've had • making generalizations about groups of people	
12	**Money matters** 3B page 117	• say what you'd do in a hypothetical situation • report what someone said to you • describe similarities/differences	• unreal conditional • reported speech • conjunctions: *both/neither, either*	• money • guessing meaning from context clues • dealing with difficult questions	

READING/WRITING	LISTENING	COMMUNICATION/PRONUNCIATION
Reading texts: • personality profiles • an article about Tiffany's **Writing tasks:** • write about your typical Saturday • write an email to a friend	**Listening tasks:** • recognize subject matter • identify key information	**Communication:** talk about your learning needs and abilities **Pronunciation:** vowel sounds /u/, /ə/, /ʌ/
Reading texts: • an article about Lady Gaga • an article about music and the brain • biographies of three Latin pop singers **Writing task:** write a short biography of a partner	**Listening tasks:** • discern details • identify main ideas	**Communication:** explain why you like a piece of music **Pronunciation:** past-tense -ed endings
Reading texts: • an article about a celebrity chef • an email invitation • a report on a study about how we rate food **Writing task:** write an email invitation	**Listening tasks:** • recognize main ideas • determine actions and plans • identify foods	**Communication:** contribute to a simple discussion **Pronunciation:** silent letters
Reading texts: • an article about extreme adventurers • an article about England **Writing task:** write a thank you note	**Listening tasks:** • confirm a prediction • identify key information • discern main ideas • recognize decisions	**Communication:** agree on choices with a partner **Pronunciation:** sentence stress
Reading texts: • a profile of a young Chinese woman • an online personal profile **Writing task:** write a personal profile	**Listening tasks:** • recognize main ideas • identify importance of biographical details	**Communication:** make a simple informal presentation **Pronunciation:** used to/didn't use to
Reading texts: • an article about New Zealand tourism • a brochure about a prison garden program **Writing task:** write a description of your favorite place	**Listening tasks:** • label a map • understand important details • check predictions • identify a decision	**Communication:** explain your preference for a vacation destination **Pronunciation:** reductions
Reading texts: • an article about an actress and body image • a guide to determining personality type • a quiz about stress **Writing task:** letters requesting and giving advice	**Listening tasks:** • match descriptions to pictures • recognize main ideas • identify "problems"	**Communication:** understand and talk about a magazine quiz **Pronunciation:** choice questions with or
Reading texts: • an article with tips on "slowing down" • a letter describing "speed dating" • jokes **Writing task:** write a story	**Listening tasks:** • understand the gist • discern details	**Communication:** talk for an extended period on a familiar topic **Pronunciation:** rising and falling intonation in questions
Reading texts: • advice for a successful job interview • an article about Mark Zuckerberg **Writing task:** write a "news article"	**Listening tasks:** • distinguish between true and false information • understand the gist and analyze details	**Communication:** take part in a simple negotiation **Pronunciation:** word stress
Reading texts: • an article about children raised by wild animals • opinions on the pros and cons of zoos • information on animal protection organizations **Writing task:** write opinions on issues	**Listening tasks:** • distinguish between true and false information • identify key words • identify sounds	**Communication:** participate in making a group decision **Pronunciation:** sentence stress
Reading texts: • an excerpt from a travel diary • advice for business travelers **Writing tasks:** • explain your choice in a travel companion • write about a place you have traveled to	**Listening tasks:** • determine differences • identify questions • determine important details • identify key travel-related words	**Communication:** achieve your goals in a typical travel conversation **Pronunciation:** past perfect contractions
Reading texts: • results of a survey about cheating • an article about a lawsuit over a baseball **Writing task:** write a formal letter	**Listening tasks:** • understand the main ideas • verify answers • determine key points	**Communication:** make a simple complaint in a store/restaurant **Pronunciation:** both, either, and neither

How much do you know . . . ?

1 Do you know these grammar terms? Complete the chart with the <u>underlined</u> words from sentences below.

1. She is <u>a</u> doctor.
2. <u>They</u> are very generous.
3. This book is <u>yours</u>.
4. <u>Does</u> she eat meat?
5. You <u>can</u> smoke outside.
6. Keith <u>has written</u> four novels.
7. How much <u>water</u> do you drink every day?
8. Could you give this <u>pen</u> to him?
9. This watch is <u>cheaper</u> than the last one.
10. <u>He's</u> very late.

a. pronoun	*They* (sentence 2)
b. count noun	
c. comparative	
d. possessive	
e. modal verb	
f. auxiliary verb	
g. contraction	
h. noncount noun	
i. article	
j. present perfect	

2 Do you know these parts of speech? Complete the chart with the correct words from the box.

> write   sister   carefully   give up   at   beautiful

Part of speech	Example	Part of speech	Example
1. noun		4. adjective	
2. verb	*write*	5. adverb	
3. phrasal verb		6. preposition	

3 Do you know these pronunciation terms? Look at the words in the box and answer the questions below about each word.

> sister   factory   chocolate

1. How many syllables are there?   2. Where's the main stress?

4 **Pair Work** Do you know this classroom language? Match questions to the replies below. Then practice with a partner.

1. What does "party animal" mean?
2. How do you spell "exercise"?
3. Can you say that again, please?
4. What page is that on?
5. Could you speak up a bit, please?
6. What's the answer to number 5?
7. What's our homework?
8. How do you pronounce the second word?

a. Page 13, at the end of Unit 1.
b. Do exercises 3, 4, and 5 on page 64.
c. I don't know. Ask Mario. He's good at grammar.
d. /ˈresɪpiz/
e. E-X-E-R-C-I-S-E
f. It's someone who likes going to parties.
g. Of course. It's really noisy in here.
h. Sure, no problem. All of it or just the last part?

UNIT 1
Your day

Warm Up

1 Find a verb phrase in the box for each photo. Then write *D* next to the things you do every day. Write *W* next to the things you do only on weekends. Write *S* next to the things you sometimes do. Write *N* next to the things you never do.

____ sleep in	____ get up early	____ talk on the phone	____ listen to music
____ watch TV	____ go to bed late	____ check your email	____ go out for dinner
____ exercise	____ text friends	____ catch a bus/train	____ read a book
____ do nothing	____ go for a walk	____ have breakfast/lunch/dinner	

2 **Pair Work** Compare with a partner. *I talk on the phone every day. How about you?*

Speaking

1 Match the pictures A–C in the questionnaire below with these descriptions.

_____ 1. This person likes staying in, eating, and watching television.

_____ 2. This person likes going out, dancing, and meeting friends.

_____ 3. This person likes reading and going to museums and art galleries.

2a **Pair Work** Ask your partner the questions below and fill in the quiz for him or her.

b Compare your results. Discuss.

What kind of **person** are you?

A

① Choose the *best* answer.

It's your birthday. Do you . . .
- ○ A go out with friends?
- ○ B have dinner at a restaurant with friends?
- ○ C get a DVD and a pizza?

② It's a sunny weekend. Do you . . .
- ○ A have a picnic with family and friends?
- ○ B visit another city?
- ○ C read a magazine at home?

③ It's your lunch break at work. Do you . . .
- ○ A go to the gym?
- ○ B go to lunch with friends?
- ○ C have a sandwich at your desk?

④ It's your summer vacation. Do you . . .
- ○ A go out at night?
- ○ B go sightseeing?
- ○ C lie on the beach?

⑤ You go shopping on vacation. Do you buy . . .
- ○ A some clothes for the evening?
- ○ B a book about the place you're in?
- ○ C ice cream?

B

C

Mostly "A"s:

You're a real party animal and fun to be with. Don't forget to stop and rest sometimes!

Mostly "B"s:

You're a culture vulture and like learning new things. Don't forget to join the party sometimes!

Mostly "C"s:

You're a total couch potato and are usually on the sofa, doing nothing. Come on—get up and join the fun!

Reading

3 Read. Is each person a "party animal," a "culture vulture," or a "couch potato"?

I <u>don't like</u> getting up early on weekends, so I usually sleep in—sometimes until 10:30! I <u>love</u> to have a big bowl of ramen on Saturday mornings. I <u>can't stand</u> going to the gym, but I sometimes go for a walk in the afternoon. I <u>like</u> going to the park and just lying on the grass and doing nothing. I'<u>m not into</u> going out on Saturday night. I stay in and talk on the phone and watch TV.

Nobu Suzuki, Tokyo, Japan

I <u>really hate</u> doing nothing, so I get up early on Saturdays and start the day by texting friends. I <u>really like</u> to meet friends for breakfast, so I catch a bus into town. After breakfast, my friends and I sometimes go to an art gallery. I'<u>m into</u> most kinds of art, so I <u>don't mind</u> which gallery we go to. I do different things on Saturday nights. I sometimes have dinner with friends, or I stay home and read.

Lola Gutierrez, Mexico City, Mexico

American English	British English
I'm into	I'm keen on

4 **Pair Work** Ask and answer the questions.

1. What do Nobu and Lola like doing?   2. What do they dislike doing?

Grammar | likes and dislikes

5 Complete the Active Grammar box using the <u>underlined</u> phrases from Exercise 3.

Active Grammar

1. _____ to have a big bowl of ramen. ☺☺☺

2. *I really like* to meet friends. ☺☺

3. *I like* going to the park. ☺

4. _____ most kinds of art. ☺

5. _____ which gallery we go to. 😐

6. _____ going out on Saturday night. ☹

7. *I don't like* getting up early. ☹

8. _____ going to the gym. ☹☹

9. *I really hate* doing nothing. ☹☹

Use a noun or a gerund after these phrases. Some phrases also take the infinitive.

---

6 Write sentences using the cues. Don't forget to change the verb if necessary.

Ex: ☺ /watch sports on TV. | I'm into watching sports on TV. |

1. ☺☺☺ /my job.
2. ☹ /do crossword puzzles.
3. ☺☺ /swim in the ocean.
4. ☹☹ /be cold.
5. 😐 /dogs.
6. ☺ /go to the movies.
7. ☹☹ /talk on the phone in English.
8. ☺☺☺ /go dancing.

Speaking

7 **Group Work** Tell other students what kind of person you are and why.

I think I'm mostly a party animal, because I love going out with my friends.

8 Write a paragraph with the title "My Typical Saturday." Use the paragraphs in Exercise 3 to help you.

Listening

1a **Pair Work** Make these sentences true for you. Tell a partner.

1. I sleep a lot.   2. Sleep is a waste of time.   3. I can only sleep on a hard bed.

> *I don't sleep a lot—usually six hours a night.*

b ▶1.02 Listen to a TV show about sleep. Check (✓) the things you hear.

☐ adults   ☐ cats   ☐ dogs   ☐ horses   ☐ snakes
☐ babies   ☐ children   ☐ fish   ☐ old people

2 Listen again and answer the questions.

1. Who sleeps about (a) seven hours _____,
   (b) seventeen hours _____, and (c) eight hours _____ every day?
2. What is strange about the way horses sleep? _____
3. What is strange about the way fish sleep? _____
4. In one year, how many hours does the average person sleep?
   a. 2,688   b. 2,860   c. 2,680
5. In one night, how many dreams does the average person have? _____

3 **Pair Work** Discuss.

1. How often do you remember your dreams?
2. How often do you have the same dream?
3. Do you have any favorite dreams?

Vocabulary | verb-noun phrases about routine actions

4a Match the questions to the answers.

1. What time do you <u>go to bed</u>?
2. Do you <u>have a snack</u> before bed?
3. How many hours do you <u>sleep</u> each night?
4. What time do you <u>get up</u>?
5. What time do you <u>have breakfast</u>?
6. Do you <u>take a shower</u> in the morning or the evening?
7. Do you ever <u>sleep in</u>?

a. At about 7 A.M.
b. About eight hours.
c. At about 11 P.M.
d. At about 7:30 A.M., after my shower.
e. I usually take one in the morning.
f. Yes. I always sleep in on Sundays.
g. No, I hardly ever eat before bed.

b ▶1.03 Listen and check your answers.

Grammar | simple present; adverbs of frequency

5 Look at the questions and answers in Exercise 4a again. Complete the Active Grammar box with *do, does, don't,* or *doesn't.*

6 Circle the correct form.

A: *Do/Does* (1.) you fall asleep quickly?

B: Yes, I *do/does* (2.). I *don't/doesn't* (3.) listen to music, I just *go/goes* (4.) to sleep right away.

A: *Do/Does* (5.) you use an alarm clock?

B: No, I *do/don't* (6.). My mom *get/gets* (7.) up first, then she *wake/wakes* (8.) me.

A: *Do/Does* (9.) anyone in your family have strange sleep habits?

B: Yes, my brother *do/does* (10.). He *talk/talks* (11.) in his sleep, but he *don't/doesn't* (12.) wake up.

> ## Active Grammar
>
> Use the simple present to talk about routines (things you do every day) and habits (things you do often).
>
> ⊕ 1. *I usually go to bed about 10:30.*
>
> ⊖ 2. *They _____ take naps during the day.*
>
>   3. *He _____ sleep in during the week.*
>
> ⊘ 4. *_____ you wake up early?*
>
>   5. *_____ she usually have a snack before bed?*
>
> **Adverbs of frequency**
>
> *never, hardly ever, sometimes, often, usually, always*
>
> *0% ———————————————▶ 100%*

See Reference page 16

Pronunciation | vowel sounds /u/ and /ʌ/

7a Match the vowel sounds to the <u>underlined</u> words.

/u/   /ʌ/

_____ 1. A: <u>Do</u> you take a nap during the day?
_____ 2. B: Yes, I <u>do</u>.
_____ 3. A: <u>Does</u> Jane get up early?
_____ 4. B: Yes, she <u>does</u>.

b ▶1.04 Listen and check. Practice with a partner.

Speaking

8 **Pair Work** Ask and answer the questions in Exercise 4a and Exercise 6.

> *What time do you go to bed?*   *I usually go to bed at about midnight.*

Write an email to update someone about your life

Reading

1 **Pair Work** Discuss.

   1. What do you see in the photos?

   2. What do you think this article will be about?

THE LITTLE BLUE BOX

Are you hoping someone will give you a little blue box from Tiffany's on your birthday? Do you know the history of that little blue box? It was in 1837 that 25-year-old Charles Lewis Tiffany opened Tiffany and Company in New York City. The store soon became famous for beautifully designed jewelry and large, expensive gems—and the "Tiffany Blue" box, which Tiffany introduced the year he opened the store.

 The New York City store on Fifth Avenue is still important, and it brings in almost 10 percent of Tiffany's sales. But Tiffany now has 220 stores across the Americas, Asia, and Europe and is opening new stores in China and India.

People all over the world know Tiffany Blue. The color is so important to Tiffany that the company has copyrighted it. No other store can use this shade of blue.

Tiffany is still selling many of its timeless designs. But modern artists such as Paloma Picasso and Frank Gehry are also designing jewelry for Tiffany. Whether classic or modern, though, the jewelry will always come in the little blue box.

2 Read the article and take turns asking and answering the questions.

   1. How old was Charles Tiffany when he opened the store?

   2. What year did he introduce the little blue box?

   3. Where does Tiffany have stores?

   4. What kind of jewelry does Tiffany sell?

   5. Why is Tiffany the only store that can use Tiffany Blue?

3 **Pair Work** Discuss.

   1. Would you like to shop at Tiffany? Why or why not?

   2. What are your favorite stores to shop at? Why?

Listening

4a ▶1.05 Listen to a reporter outside Tiffany's. Complete the chart.

Where are you from?	What are you doing in New York?	What are you doing at Tiffany's?
Person 1:	*visiting her sister*	
Person 2:		*looking for a ring*
Person 3:	*shopping*	

b **Pair Work** Compare your answers with a partner.

Grammar | present continuous

5 Read the Active Grammar box. How is the present continuous used in each sentence 1–6? Write *a* or *b*.

6 Circle the correct choices.

1. I *take/'m taking* a Spanish class this year. It *starts/is starting* at 7:30 on Mondays.

2. What *do you do/are you doing* these days? *Do you still study English/Are you still studying English?*

3. Yuko *doesn't eat/isn't eating* meat. She *doesn't like/isn't liking* it.

4. What *do you usually do/are you usually doing* during summer vacation?

5. They *often go/'re often going* to Costa Rica with friends.

7 ▶1.06 Listen. What is happening? Answer in complete sentences. Begin like this: *Someone is . . .*

8 SPEAKING EXCHANGE

Student A: Look at the picture on the right.
Student B: Look at the picture on page 67.
Find five more differences.

> *Is the man buying a DVD?*

> *No, he isn't. He's buying a book.*

Writing

9 Read the email in the Writing bank on page 69. Do the exercises.

10 Write an email to a friend you haven't talked to in a while. Tell him or her about your life right now.

> Hi Angela,
> How are you? I have so much to tell you . . .

Active Grammar

Use the present continuous for:

a. actions happening at this moment

b. temporary actions happening "around now" but not at this moment

⊕ _____ 1. *I'm studying engineering.*

_____ 2. *My girlfriend is shopping for clothes.*

⊖ _____ 3. *I'm not talking on the phone.*

_____ 4. *We're not exercising enough.*

? _____ 5. *Are you working in the city this week?*

_____ 6. *What are you eating?*

Use the simple present (NOT the present continuous) with stative verbs (**Ex:** *be, know, like, love,* etc.).

See Reference page 16

Review

1 Complete the conversations with the correct form of the simple present. Then practice with a partner.

Ex: A: _Do you get up_ (you/get up) early?

B: Yes, I do. On weekdays _____ (1. I/get up) at about 6:30.

_____ (2. I/go to bed) early, too.

A: _____ (3. you/go to bed) before ten o'clock?

B: No, I don't, but _____ (4. I/fall asleep) in front of the TV sometimes.

A: My brother is a very good swimmer.

B: _____ (5. he/swim) a lot?

A: Yes, he does. _____ (6. He/get up) very early and

_____ (7. swim) for two hours before breakfast. Then

_____ (8. he/go) back to the pool after work.

B: _____ (9. he/go) out with his friends much?

A: Only on weekends. _____ (10. He/not/go) out during the week at all.

2 Complete the conversations using the present continuous form of the verbs in the box.

~~do~~   have   sit   check   watch   go   listen

Ex: A: What _are you doing_ (you) right now?

B: I _____ (1.) on a bus with some friends. We _____ (2.)

downtown. What about you?

A: I _____ (3.) lunch with my family.

B: _____ (4. Jack) TV?

A: No, he isn't. He _____ (5.) to music and _____ (6.)

his email.

3 Circle the correct choice to complete each sentence.

Ex: I (usually go)/am usually going to work by car.

1. Listen to that man. What language _does he speak/is he speaking_?

2. It _doesn't rain/isn't raining_ much in the summer here.

3. You _work/'re working_ very hard today.

4. _Do you prefer/Are you preferring_ tea or coffee?

5. I _stay/'m staying_ at the W Hotel in Montreal for a week.

6. Who's that woman? What _does she want/is she wanting_?

Communication | talk about your learning needs and abilities

4 Look at the Wheel of English. Match the words and phrases in the box to the pictures.

~~grammar~~   vocabulary   reading   writing   listening   speaking

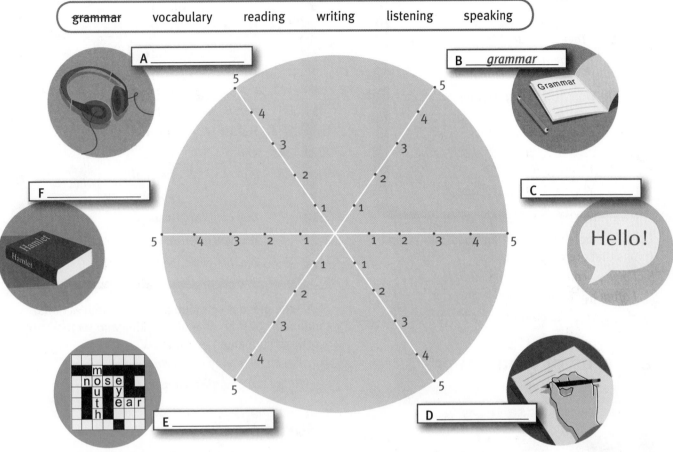

A _____

B _____*grammar*_____

F _____

C _____

Hello!

E _____

D _____

5 ▶1.07 Listen. How important is each aspect of English for Antonio? Write an ✗ at the correct place on each part of the wheel. 1 is not important; 5 is very important.

6 Listen again. How good is Antonio at each aspect of English? Make notes.

7 **Pair Work** Complete your own Wheel of English. Then explain it to your partner. Use language from the How To box.

How To:

Talk about your learning needs and abilities

Say what's important to you	*Grammar is (very/pretty) important to me.* *Reading is not (very) important to me.*
Say what you are good at	*I'm (very/pretty) good at listening.*

8 **Group Work** What are your strategies for learning English? Do you listen to an English language radio station? Do you keep a vocabulary notebook? Compare. Make notes about the best strategies you hear.

> *I like to write new vocabulary words on notes and put them on my refrigerator. That way I see them a couple of times a day.*

Unit 1 Reference

Simple present

⊕ ⊖	I/You/We/They	go don't go	to bed early.
	He/She/It	goes doesn't go	
❓	Do	you/we/they get up	early?
	Does	he/she/it get up	

Yes, I do./No, I don't.

Yes, he does./No, he doesn't.

Use the simple present for routines, habits, and things that are generally true.

I always call my parents on Sundays.

I often go to the movies.

He doesn't like going to bed.

Adverbs of frequency

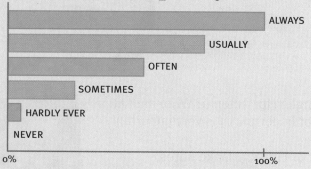

Use adverbs of frequency to say how often you do something.

I usually play tennis on Saturday.

The adverb of frequency comes after the verb *be*.

I'm never late.

The adverb of frequency comes before a main verb.

He sometimes goes out on Saturdays.

Use the affirmative with *never* and *hardly ever*, not the negative.

He hardly ever gets up early.

Present continuous

⊕	I	am	working.
	He/She/It	is	
	We/You/They	are	
⊖	I	am not	
	He/She/It	is not	
	You/We/They	are not	
❓	Am	I	sleeping in?
	Is	he/she/it	
	Are	you/we/they	

Yes, I am./No, I'm not.

Yes, you are./No, you aren't.

Yes, he is./No, he's not (he isn't).

Use the present continuous to talk about actions happening at the time of speaking and temporary actions happening around now.

I'm checking my email right now.

He's taking English classes this year.

Stative verbs

like	hate	prefer	understand
love	know	believe	remember
need	want		

Use the simple present (NOT the present continuous) with stative verbs.

I know how to play chess.

Unit Vocabulary

Verb-noun phrases about daily routine

read	go to the gym	talk on the phone
sleep	get up early	go out for dinner
wake up	do nothing	go to bed late
watch TV	have a snack	lie on the beach
exercise	go for a walk	meet some friends
take a nap	have a picnic	catch a bus/train
sleep in	take a shower	check your email
fall asleep	listen to music	
have breakfast/lunch/dinner		

UNIT 2
Musical tastes

A

B

C

D

Warm Up

1 What musical instruments can you see in the photos? Match the photos (A–D) to words in the box. What other instruments do you know?

> harp   violin   piano   trumpet   electric guitar
> cello   flute   drums   saxaphone

2 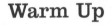 **Pair Work** Look at the types of music listed below. Try to name an artist or song for each type of music.

> classical   Latin   rock   hip hop   pop   jazz

3 **Group Work** Work in small groups. Discuss.

1. What kinds of music do you like? What kinds do you dislike?
2. Who's your favorite singer, band, or composer?
3. What was the last concert you went to? How was it?
4. How often do you download music from the Internet?
5. Do you play a musical instrument? When did you learn?

> *I download music from the Internet almost every week.*

> *Really? I hardly ever do. I still buy CDs.*

Reading

1 Read the article and answer the questions below.

Gaga for Lady Gaga

Before Lady Gaga's first album hit the music scene in 2008, she was an unknown 22-year-old singer-songwriter. The album, *The Fame*, brought three number-one hits, five Grammy nominations, and sudden worldwide fame for Lady Gaga. Many people were surprised at her unusual clothes (many of which she makes herself), crazy hairstyles, and wild concerts (she calls them "performance art"). But her fans love them, along with her very danceable music.

1. How old was Lady Gaga when she became famous?
2. Who writes her music?
3. Who makes a lot of her clothes?
4. What does she call her concerts?

Listening

2a ▶1.08 Listen to a short biography of Lady Gaga.

Student A: Answer the odd-numbered questions in the chart (1, 3, 5, etc.).

Student B: Answer the even-numbered questions in the chart (2, 4, 6, etc.).

1. When was she born?	
2. When did she begin performing?	
3. Where did she go to school?	
4. Was she a good student?	
5. Where did she go to college?	
6. What kind of job did she get with Sony?	
7. Where did she move in 2008?	
8. What did she finish in 2008?	

b **Pair Work** Complete the chart by taking turns asking and answering the questions you *didn't* answer. Then listen again and check your answers.

Grammar | simple past

3a Complete the Active Grammar box with the correct form of the verb in the simple past.

b Which verbs in the Active Grammar box are regular? Which are irregular?

Active Grammar

Use the simple past for completed actions in the past.

➕ 1. She _____ her name. (change)

➖ 2. She _____ at school. (fit in)

❓ 3. Where _____ she _____ ? (move)

See Reference page 26 and irregular verb chart on page 72

4 Complete the dialog with the simple past of the verbs in parentheses. Then practice the dialog with a partner.

A: Where _____ (1. you/grow up)?

B: When I _____ (2. be) very young, we _____ (3. live) in Miami. Then when I was 12, my family _____ (4. move) to Chicago. I _____ (5. not/like) it at first, but when I was a teenager, I _____ (6. love) it.

A: _____ (7. you/go) to college when you _____ (8. graduate)?

B: No. I _____ (9. not/go) to college until I was 22. First, I _____ (10. get) a job in a clothing store for a year and _____ (11. save) up some money. Then I _____ (12. travel). After that, I _____ (13. go) to college.

Pronunciation | past tense *-ed* endings

5a ▶1·09 Listen and repeat.

> worked   believed   ended   moved   wanted   loved   finished   waited   kissed

b Put the verbs in the correct column, according to the pronunciation of *-ed*.

/t/	/d/	/ɪd/
worked		

Speaking

6 **Pair Work** Interview your partner about his or her life. Use the ideas below and the language in the How To box to help you. Take notes. Ask:

- when/where he or she was born
- where he or she grew up
- what he or she liked/disliked about school
- what job he or she wanted to do
- what important things happened as a teenager
- what he or she did when he or she graduated
- what important things happened after that

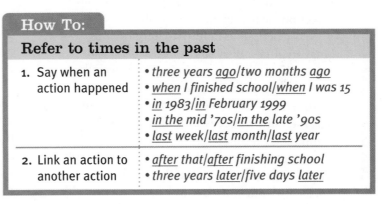

How To:

Refer to times in the past	
1. Say when an action happened	• *three years <u>ago</u>/two months <u>ago</u>* • <u>*when*</u> *I finished school/*<u>*when*</u> *I was 15* • *in 1983/*<u>*in*</u> *February 1999* • <u>*in the mid '70s*</u>*/*<u>*in the late '90s*</u> • <u>*last*</u> *week/*<u>*last*</u> *month/*<u>*last*</u> *year*
2. Link an action to another action	• <u>*after*</u> *that/*<u>*after*</u> *finishing school* • *three years <u>later</u>/five days <u>later</u>*

Writing

7 Write a short biography of your partner. Use your notes from Exercise 6.

> Paula was born in 1990. She grew up in a small town near Bogota. She didn't like school, but she loved music . . .

Reading

1 **Pair Work** Think about three of your favorite songs. How does each one make you feel? Tell a partner using the adjectives in the box and your own words.

happy	sad	relaxed
awake	sleepy	thoughtful

"What a Wonderful World" made me feel relaxed and happy.

2 Read the article. Mark the statements below true (*T*), false (*F*), or don't know (*?*).

The Mozart Effect

Music is not just entertainment. It is medicine for both the brain and the body. Don Campbell is an expert on *the Mozart effect* and the amazing power of music. He says that all kinds of music, from Mozart to jazz, from Latin to rock, can affect our learning and our health.

Many people use music to help them feel relaxed after a busy day at work. Music can also reduce the stress of being ill, especially by reducing pain. The director of Baltimore Hospital says that 30 minutes of classical music has the same effect as 10 milligrams of the painkiller Valium.

Campbell also says that music can help you concentrate, but you need the right kind of music for your mood. And he says you should listen for about ten minutes before you start studying. If your mind needs relaxing, or you are underline{tired} and you want to feel more underline{energetic}, you should choose the appropriate music to help you. You can use many different kinds of music to help you concentrate. Mozart's music is very popular, however, because it is very organized, and it makes your brain more alert and underline{imaginative}.

Music helps you study, and it can actually make you more underline{intelligent}. In one study, students who listened to Mozart before doing a test scored higher than those who didn't. Many studies also show that children who learn to play a musical instrument before the age of 12 can remember information better for the rest of their lives.

_____ 1. Music is good for our bodies and brains.

_____ 2. Don Campbell loves Mozart's music.

_____ 3. Many hospitals use music to help with pain.

_____ 4. Only Mozart's music helps you to study.

_____ 5. The students listened to Mozart for 15 minutes before doing the test.

_____ 6. It's a good idea for children to learn to play a musical instrument.

3 **Pair Work** Discuss.

1. What music do you listen to?   2. What effect does it have?

20

Vocabulary | word families

4a Match the <u>underlined</u> adjectives in the article on page 20 with the definitions below.

1. _____ = good at learning and understanding things
2. _____ = can think of new and interesting ideas
3. _____ = active and can work hard
4. _____ = calm and not worried
5. _____ = feeling that you want to rest or sleep

b Complete the table. Use a dictionary if necessary.

5 ▶1.10 Listen and <u>underline</u> the main stress in the words in the table.

1. Can you figure out any rules for word stress with nouns?
2. Which pairs of words have the same stress?
3. Which pairs have different stress?

Adjective	Noun
relaxed	*relaxation*
energetic	
imaginative	
intelligent	

6 Circle the correct choice to complete each sentence.

1. Latin music makes me feel *energetic/energy*.
2. I'm a very *imaginative/imagination* person.
3. I need to use my *imaginative/imagination* in my job.
4. Everyone has the *intelligent/intelligence* to learn a language.
5. I listen to music in the morning to give me *energetic/energy*.
6. Jazz makes me feel *relaxed/relaxation*.

7 **Pair Work** Use the words in Exercise 6 to make sentences about yourself.

> *Going for a run makes me feel energetic.*

Grammar | agreement: *so* and *neither*

8a Complete the Active Grammar box.

b **Pair Work** Cover the answers and practice the conversations from the Active Grammar box.

Speaking

9 **Pair Work** Use the phrases in the box to make sentences about music. Respond to your partner's comments.

> I have . . .   I really like . . .   I'm . . .
> I think . . .   I don't like . . .
> I'm not . . .   I sometimes go . . .

> *I really like going to see musicals.*   *So do I.*

Active Grammar

Same

1. **A:** *I like rock music.*   **B:** *So do I.*
2. **A:** *I'm not into him.*   **B:** *Neither _____ I.*
3. **A:** *I didn't go.*   **B:** *Neither _____ I.*

Different

4. **A:** *I usually listen to rock music.*   **B:** *I don't.*
5. **A:** *I can't play an instrument.*   **B:** *I _____.*
6. **A:** *I don't like loud music.*   **B:** *I _____.*

See Reference page 26

Enrique Iglesias

Alejandro Sanz

Marc Anthony

Speaking

1 **Pair Work** Discuss.
   1. Do you like Latin pop? Why or why not?
   2. What do you know about the singers pictured here?

2a **SPEAKING EXCHANGE** Work in groups of three. Read about one of the singers above.
   Student A: Read the biographical information on page 67.
   Student B: Read the biographical information on page 68 - bottom.
   Student C: Read the biographical information on page 68 - top.

  b Ask your partners the questions below. Then guess which singer each partner is describing.
   1. What kind of music does he sing?
   2. How many albums has he released?
   3. Have any of his albums been in English?
   4. What music awards has he won?
   5. Is he married?
   6. Who are his parents?

Grammar | present perfect and simple past

3 Read the examples in the Active Grammar box. Then complete the rules by writing *present perfect* or *simple past*.

Active Grammar

He grew up in Miami.
He has released over nine albums.
When was he born?
Has he been in any movies?

1. Use the _____ to talk about an action or experience at a specific time in the past.

2. Use the _____ to talk about an action or experience in the past when the time is not important or not known.

See Reference page 26

4a Complete the conversations with the present perfect or simple past.

A: _____ (1. you/ever/win) a competition?

B: Yes, I _____ (2.). I _____ (3. win) a singing competition when I was six.

A: _____ (4. you/watch) TV last night?

B: Yes, I _____ (5.). I _____ (6. see) a documentary about global warming.

A: _____ (7. you/ever/meet) a famous person?

B: No, I _____ (8.). But I _____ (9. see) Madonna in concert last year!

A: _____ (10. you/ever/play) a musical instrument in public?

B: Yes, I _____ (11.). I _____ (12. be) in a band when I was a teenager.

b ▶1.11 Listen and check your answers.

c **Pair Work** Ask and answer the questions in Exercise 4a.

Vocabulary | achievements

5a Match the verbs from A with the phrases from B.

A	B
_____ 1. learn	a. a prize for (dancing/a sport)
_____ 2. give	b. to speak another language
_____ 3. start	c. a difficult test
_____ 4. win	d. your own company
_____ 5. pass	e. an article/a book
_____ 6. write	f. a speech to (30 people)

b **Pair Work** Which of the above have you done/not done? Which other achievements are you most proud of in your life? Tell your partner.

> I've played the piano in a concert.
> I'm really proud of that.

Speaking

6 **Group Work** Work in groups of three. Tell your partners about a singer or musician that you like. Use the questions in Exercise 2b as a guide. Your partners guess who you are talking about.

Review

1 Complete the sentences using the simple past.

> **Ex:** I _*learned*_ to play the piano when I was a child.
>
> My father _*taught*_ me. (learn/teach)

1. He _____ his old computer and _____ a new one. (sell/buy)
2. My grandmother _____ and _____ her arm. (fall/break)
3. I was on a diet last week. I _____ only fruit and I _____ only water. (eat/drink)
4. When we _____ on vacation last year, I _____ a lot of photos. (be/take)
5. I _____ to a concert last night and _____ two really good bands. (go/see)

2 Complete the dialogs with the simple past of the verbs in the boxes. Then practice with a partner.

> | ~~do~~ | say | think |
> |------|------|----------|
> | go | meet | not/like |

> | stop | like | not/like |
> |------|------|----------|
> | hate | be | live |

A: What _*did you do*_ (you) last weekend?

B: On Friday night, I _____ (1.) my friend Natalia and we _____ (2.) to see a movie. I _____ (3.) it was a really good film, but Natalia _____ (4.) it. She _____ (5.) it was boring.

A: Where _____ (6. you) born?

B: In Canada. I _____ (7.) in Vancouver when I was a child.

A: _____ (8. you) it?

B: No, I _____ (9.) it. I _____ (10.) the weather because it never _____ (11.) raining!

3 Agree or disagree using *so*, *neither*, or short answers. Then practice with a partner.

> **Ex:** **A:** I have a headache.
>
> **B:** (agree) _*So do I*_ .

1. **A:** I thought that coat was very expensive.
   B: (agree) _____ .
2. **A:** I didn't like her last single.
   B: (disagree) _____ .
3. **A:** I'm doing my homework at the moment.
   B: (agree) _____ .
4. **A:** I don't go swimming much.
   B: (agree) _____ .

4 Complete the sentences using the present perfect.

> **Ex:** Susie _*has seen*_ *Avatar* five times! (see)

1. I _____ of that band. (not hear)
2. _____ a marathon? (you/ever/run)
3. I _____ to Carnival in Brazil twice. (be)
4. _____ your leg? (you/ever/break)
5. She's nervous because she _____ a horse before. (not ride)
6. _____ any climbing before? (you/do)
7. I _____ all over the world. (work)
8. _____ music from the Internet? (you/ever/download)

Communication | explain why you like a piece of music

5 ▶1.12 You're going to hear a radio show. Listen to the introduction. What is the show about?

6a ▶1.13 Listen to the rest of the show and complete the chart.

Piece of music	Artist	Reason
3		
2		
1		

b Compare your answers with a partner.

7a Complete the sentences from the listening, using the phrases in the box.

> reminds me of (a time/a place/a person . . .)
> makes me (feel happy/cry/smile . . .)
> remember (listening/going/feeling . . .)

1. This music _____ great.
2. It _____ when I was in college.
3. When I first heard it, it _____ because it was so beautiful.
4. I _____ to this song when I was on vacation in Spain.

b ▶1.14 Listen and check your answers. Repeat the sentences.

8a Choose your top three pieces of music. Complete the chart.

Piece of music	Artist	Reason
3		
2		
1		

b **Group Work** Tell other students about your choices. Use your notes and the language from Exercise 7a.

> *It's hard, but I guess my number three choice is "I Gotta Feeling" by The Black Eyed Peas. It always makes me feel happy.*

Unit 2 Reference

Simple past

Regular verbs

➕	I played jazz music all day yesterday.
➖	He didn't finish his exam.
❓	Why did you wait so long? Did you like the last Coldplay CD?
	Yes, I did./No, I didn't.

Irregular verbs

➕	I left Los Angeles in 1993.
➖	They didn't come home last night.
❓	Where did she grow up? Did he go to school with you?
	Yes, he did./No, he didn't.

Use the simple past to talk about completed actions.

Use the same form for all persons (but *was/were* for the verb *be*).

Add *-ed* to regular verbs to make the past form.

Use *didn't (did not)* to make the negative.

so and *neither*

		Agree/Disagree
➕	I like chocolate.	So do I./I don't.
	I hated swimming.	So did I./I didn't.
	I'm a student.	So am I./I'm not.
	I was into pop.	So was I./I wasn't.
		Agree/Disagree
➖	I don't watch TV.	Neither do I./I do.
	I didn't go out.	Neither did I./I did.
	I'm not enjoying it.	Neither am I./I am.
	I wasn't late.	Neither was I./I was.

Use *so* and *neither* to say that you agree with or have the same experience as someone.

Affirmative statement: use *so* + affirmative auxiliary.

Negative statement: use *neither* + affirmative auxiliary.

Use the opposite auxiliary to say that you disagree with or have a different experience from someone.

Present perfect

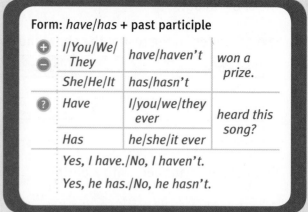

➕ ➖	I/You/We/They	have/haven't	won a prize.
	She/He/It	has/hasn't	
❓	Have	I/you/we/they ever	heard this song?
	Has	he/she/it ever	
	Yes, I have./No, I haven't.		
	Yes, he has./No, he hasn't.		

Form: *have/has* + past participle

Use the present perfect to talk about an action or experience in the general past—the specific time is not important or is not known.

Don't use the present perfect with past time expressions (*last night, two weeks ago*).

Use the simple past to talk about an action or experience at a specific time in the past.

A: *I've visited 11 countries in my life.*
B: *Have you ever been to Asia?*
A: *Yes, I have. I went to Thailand in 2001.*

Unit Vocabulary

Music

pop	jazz	hip hop
rock	Latin	composer
band	singer	classical

release an album
download music from the Internet

Word families (adjective/noun)

energetic/energy	imaginative/imagination
relaxed/relaxation	intelligent/intelligence

Achievements

give a speech	start your own company
win a prize	write an article/a book
graduate	pass a difficult test

learn to speak another language

For a list of irregular verbs, see page 72.

Warm Up

1 What foods can you see in the photos?

2 Complete the sentences using the words or phrases in the box.

> cook for yourself   ~~give up eating~~   eat out   celebrity chefs   diets   vegetarian

Ex: Is there any food that you would like to _give up eating_____? If so, why?

1. Have you ever been a _____? Why or why not?

2. Do you know any special _____ for people who want to lose weight fast?

3. Do you _____ very often? Do you follow recipes?

4. How often do you _____? What kind of restaurants do you like?

5. Are there any famous _____ in your country?

Reading

1 Read the article and then answer the questions below.

"WE NEED TO MAKE SURE THAT ... ARE GIVEN TH... OPPO... TO LEARN ABOU... FOO... E STILL YOUNG, W... ...RE SORTED ... OLIVER"

Jamie Oliver

Food lovers everywhere love the celebrity chef Jamie Oliver. One big reason is his simple, easy, and above all tasty recipes, which he has put together in some excellent cookbooks. Good food was always very important in Jamie's family. His parents had a pub in the south-east of England, and from the age of eight he started cooking and helping the chefs.

Not long ago, he started a new project. He opened a restaurant called "15" in East London. He gave himself nine months to take a team of unemployed 16 to 24-year-olds with almost no previous cooking experience and turn them into top-class chefs. Jamie says his biggest lesson is that each individual needs a different approach. Some people learn quickly, and others need a little more time.

The project also became a TV series called *Jamie's Kitchen*, which millions of people watched. One of the real success stories was KerryAnn Dunlop. Originally, she didn't get into college, but after Jamie took her on, everything changed.

Now she runs her own section of the kitchen. "Everyone is still having a really good time. We get tired sometimes, but we have fun in the kitchen, and seeing everyone enjoying the meals we've prepared makes us all feel good." And about Jamie, she says, "He's fantastic. He's like a big brother or best friend to me now."

So what is she going to do next? "I think I'd like to work abroad. I'm going to apply for a job in a top New York restaurant."

1. Why is Jamie Oliver's food successful?
2. When did Jamie start cooking?
3. Who did Jamie employ as chefs?
4. What is surprising about KerryAnn's story?
5. How does she feel about Jamie?
6. Where would she like to work next?

2a Match a word or phrase from **A** with a word from **B** to make phrases from the article.

A	B
a real success ____*story*____	restaurant
top-class _____	~~story~~
no previous _____	chef
open a _____	abroad
tasty _____	experience
work _____	recipe

b **Pair Work** Take turns making sentences about Jamie or KerryAnn using the phrases above.

> *KerryAnn is one of the real success stories of the project.*

Grammar | *be going to*: future

3 ▶1.15 Listen to this trainee chef talk about her future plans. Then answer the questions.

1. What are her plans for the summer?
2. What are her plans after that?

4 Listen again and complete the sentences in the Active Grammar box.

5 Correct the sentences below. There is a word missing in each sentence.

                   'm
   Ex: I going to be an astronaut when I grow up.

1. They're going visit their son in Australia in the summer.
2. What he going to do this afternoon?
3. You going to see Sarah this weekend?
4. We're going to tennis on Sunday morning.
5. They not going to work abroad this summer.
6. When are you to visit me?
7. Ann isn't going catch the train.

6 **Pair Work** Tell your partner three things you plan to do this week—two true things and one false. Your partner must decide which is false.

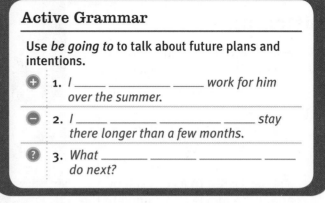

Active Grammar

Use *be going to* to talk about future plans and intentions.

➕ 1. I _____ _____ ____ work for him over the summer.

➖ 2. I _____ _____ _____ ____ stay there longer than a few months.

❓ 3. What _____ _____ _____ ____ do next?

See Reference page 36

Speaking

7a What are your plans for the next two years? Think about these areas of your life and make notes.

work	travel	hobbies and sports
home	education	friends and family

    Work — change my job / earn more money

    Travel — visit China / see the Great Wall

b **Pair Work** Talk about your future plans. Use the How To box to help you.

How To:

Talk about future plans	
1. Ask someone about their plans	*What are your plans for the next two years?*
2. • Describe your plans	*I'm going to learn English . . . I'm going to get a new job . . .*
• Give a time reference	*. . . this year . . . next year*
• Give a reason	*. . . because I want to work abroad. . . . to earn some money.*

Write an informal invitation

GRAMMAR defining relative clauses

CAN DO ✓

Listening

1 **Pair Work** Look at the photo from the movie *Big Night*. Discuss.

1. What nationality do you think the two men are?

2. What do you think the movie might be about?

2 ▶1.16 Listen to a conversation about the movie and complete the notes below.

1. *Name of film:*
   It's called <u>Big Night</u>.

2. *Time/place:*
   It's set in _____
   _____.

3. *Main characters:*
   It's about _____
   _____.

4. *Problem:*
   The problem is that _____
   _____.

5. *The plan:*
   The plan is that _____.

3 **Pair Work** Think of a movie you like. Make notes as in Exercise 2. Tell your partner about the movie. Use the phrases above.

> *I saw a great movie recently. It's called . . .*

Pronunciation | silent letters

4a Cross out the silent letters in the words below.

knife	island	spaghetti	comfortable	Wednesday
lamb	whistle	vegetable	chocolate	

b ▶1.17 Listen and repeat. Then check your answers.

5 ▶1.18 **Pair Work** Listen. Then read the sentences to your partner.

1. I had lamb for lunch on Wednesday.

2. Would you prefer vegetable soup or spaghetti?

3. Chocolate makes me feel calm.

4. The house on the island is very comfortable.

5. Don't forget to bring a whistle and a knife.

Grammar | relative clauses

6 Look at the examples and complete the Active Grammar box with the <u>underlined</u> words.

> *It's about two brothers <u>who</u> live in New York.*
>
> *They own a restaurant <u>that</u> isn't doing very well.*
>
> *Next door there's a restaurant <u>where</u> they serve terrible Italian food.*

See Reference page 36

7 **Pair Work** Take turns making sentences from the prompts.

> **Ex:** The news channel/I like the best/CNN.

> *The news channel that I like the best is CNN.*

1. Spinach/the only vegetable/I never eat.
2. The place/I feel happiest/my bedroom.
3. The town/I was born/beautiful.
4. My sister/the only person/looks like me.
5. The music/I listen to the most/jazz.
6. The thing/I like the most about myself/my hair.

Speaking

8 **SPEAKING EXCHANGE** Read the How To box. Then practice describing things to your partner. **Student A:** Look at page 67. **Student B:** Look at page 68.

How To:

Describe something you don't know the name of	
Describe a count noun	*It's the thing that you use for eating cereal.* (spoon)
Describe a noncount noun	*It's the stuff that you put on pasta.* (sauce)
Describe a person	*It's the person who takes your food order.* (waiter)

Writing

9 Read the message below. Then look at the Writing bank on pages 69–70.

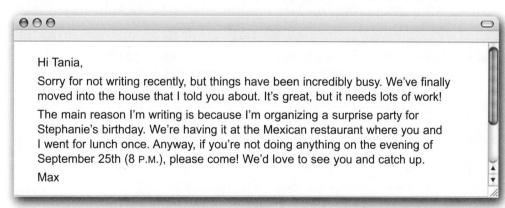

Hi Tania,

Sorry for not writing recently, but things have been incredibly busy. We've finally moved into the house that I told you about. It's great, but it needs lots of work!

The main reason I'm writing is because I'm organizing a surprise party for Stephanie's birthday. We're having it at the Mexican restaurant where you and I went for lunch once. Anyway, if you're not doing anything on the evening of September 25th (8 P.M.), please come! We'd love to see you and catch up.

Max

10 Write a short message to a friend. Give recent news and invite him or her to a party.

Vocabulary | sensory adjectives and verbs

1 Mark the adjectives positive (+) or negative (–).

_____ delicious   _____ tasteless   _____ tasty   _____ disgusting   _____ mouth-watering   _____ awful

2 Match the sentences to the pictures below.

_____ 1. This **tastes** delicious!   _____ 4. You **feel** hot!

_____ 2. You **look** nice!   _____ 5. This doesn't **smell** great.

_____ 3. That **sounds** awful!

3 **Pair Work** Use _look, sound, smell, taste,_ and _feel_ to give your opinion about the following.

fresh coffee	violins	being in love	diamonds
your shoes	old milk	chili peppers	cigarettes

Fresh coffee smells wonderful, especially in the morning.

Reading

4 Read the article and circle the correct meaning of the <u>underlined</u> words or phrases in the text.

The Best Meal You Ever Had

For a great meal, which is more important—the food you eat or where you eat it? An article in _The Week_ magazine suggests that where one eats may be more important than the food itself. Professor John Edwards and his team served chicken à la king—a chicken, mushroom, and cream sauce dish served over rice—to people in ten different <u>locations</u>.[1] They made sure that the food was always the same by using the exact same cooks, <u>ingredients</u>,[2] and cooking methods.

Among the places they served the dish were a nursing home, an army training camp, and an expensive four-star restaurant. After the meal, the researchers asked the diners to rate the food. Diners rated the taste, <u>texture</u>,[3] and <u>appearance</u>[4] of the food on a scale from one (poor) to ten (excellent).

The researchers found that diners rated the meal the lowest at the army training camp. As one soldier remarked, "It tastes awful and smells disgusting!" The dish also got low ratings at the nursing home. However, at the four-star restaurant, diners gave the chicken à la king a very high rating and said it tasted delicious! According to Edwards, "The results show that in many cases, the location is actually much more important than the food."

1. a. times   b. places   3. how something   a. tastes   b. feels

2. a. plates   b. things that go into a dish   4. how something   a. looks   b. sounds

5 Answer the questions below.

1. Where did Edwards's team serve chicken à la king?
2. How did they make sure it was always the same?
3. What did the diners score the dish on?
4. Where did the dish get the best and worst scores?

6 **Pair Work** Discuss.

1. Is the place people eat important? Why or why not?
2. Where is your favorite place to eat?

Grammar | definite plans: present continuous

7a ▶1.19 Listen to the conversation. What is the woman doing tonight?

b Listen again and complete the Active Grammar box.

8a **Pair Work** Take turns making sentences using the present continuous.

1. I/not do/anything/tonight.
2. Karen/go to a concert/next week.
3. He/not go out/this weekend.
4. We/watch TV/at home/tonight.
5. they/spend next weekend/at the beach?
6. I/play football/tomorrow night.

b Tell your partner about your plans.

> I'm going to the movies with my friend Tomo on Saturday.

Active Grammar

Form the present continuous with: *be* + verb + *-ing*

Use the present continuous to talk about future plans that are definite (a time and place is decided).

1. What _____ you doing tonight?
2. I _____ going out for dinner with Carlos.
3. He _____ coming with us.

See Reference page 36

Speaking

9 Look at the How To box. Think of other phrases to replace the <u>underlined</u> ones.

How To: Make plans	
A Check if someone is free	<u>What are you doing on</u> Friday night?
B Reply	⊕ Nothing. Why?
	⊖ I'm sorry, but I'm busy. I'm <u>seeing Jo</u>.
A Make a suggestion	<u>Why don't we try</u> the Indian restaurant?
B Accept/reject	⊕ <u>Great idea!</u>
	⊖ <u>I'm not really into</u> Indian food.
A Arrange to meet	<u>I can meet you</u> at the restaurant at 7:00.
B Confirm	⊕ Great!
	⊖ 8:00 <u>would be better for me</u>.

10 **Group Work** Write down your schedule for next weekend. Then make plans to do something with three different classmates. Add the plans to your schedule.

Review

1 Answer the questions below with *be going to* and the word(s) in parentheses.
Then practice with a partner.

> **Ex:** Have you finished the report? *(tomorrow)*   *No, I'm going to finish it tomorrow.*

1. Have you had something to eat? (later) _____
2. Have you taken the dog for a walk? (after dinner) _____
3. Have you bought Mary a birthday present? (this weekend) _____
4. Have you painted the spare bedroom? (on Tuesday) _____

2 Make questions with *be going to* for each situation.

> **Ex:** Your friend tells you that she is going into town.
>
> What *are you going* _____ to buy?

1. Your friend says he wants to quit smoking.
   When _____ ?
2. Tom tells you that it's Jane's birthday next week.
   Are _____ a gift?

3. Your friend has bought a painting.
   _____ put it?
4. You see a friend filling a bucket with hot water.
   Are _____ car?

3 Combine the two sentences to make one sentence with a relative clause. Use *who, that,* or *where.* (You may sometimes need to leave out a word.)

> **Ex:** This is the car. I would like to buy it.   *This is the car that I would like to buy.*

1. A waiter brought our food. He was very friendly.
   The _____.
2. This is a restaurant. John asked me to marry him here.
   This _____.
3. A train goes to the airport. It runs every 20 minutes.
   The _____.
4. This is the corner. The accident happened here.
   This _____.

4 Look at Carla's schedule. Write complete sentences about her plans.

Monday	
DAY OFF!	11 A.M. dentist
	2 P.M. lunch with Jenny
	6:30 P.M. Italian class

Tuesday
10 A.M. presentation to sales reps
3 P.M. meeting with marketing director
6 P.M. call US office
8 P.M. movie with Nathan

1. *She's going to the dentist on Monday.*
2. _____
3. _____
4. _____
5. _____
6. _____
7. _____
8. _____

Communication | contribute to a simple discussion

5 **Group Work** Tell other students about one of your favorite restaurants. Describe:

- the kind and quality of food
- the service
- the kind of people who go there
- the size of the restaurant
- the prices
- the general atmosphere

6 ▶1.20 Listen to a man talking about his plans. Complete the menu.

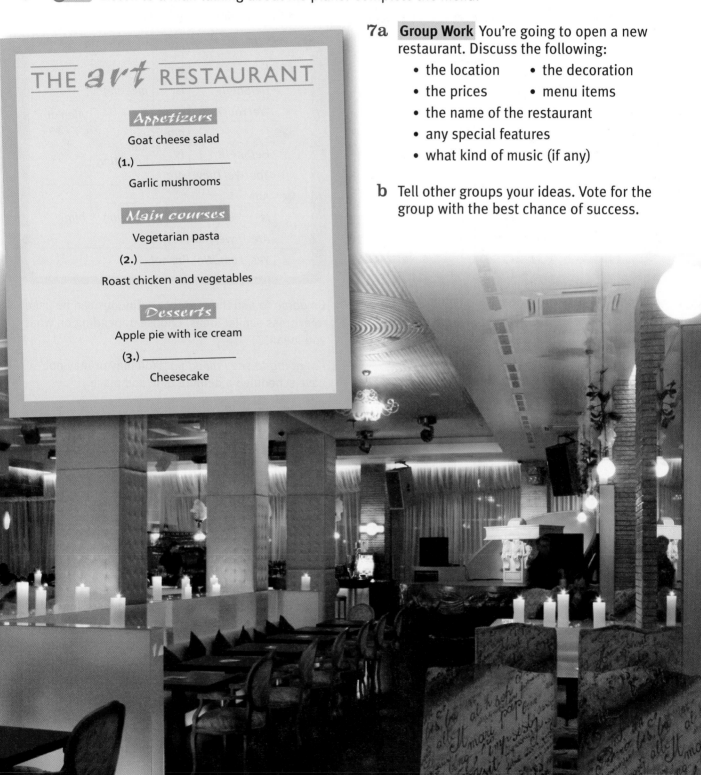

THE *art* RESTAURANT

Appetizers

Goat cheese salad

(1.) _____

Garlic mushrooms

Main courses

Vegetarian pasta

(2.) _____

Roast chicken and vegetables

Desserts

Apple pie with ice cream

(3.) _____

Cheesecake

7a **Group Work** You're going to open a new restaurant. Discuss the following:

- the location
- the decoration
- the prices
- menu items
- the name of the restaurant
- any special features
- what kind of music (if any)

b Tell other groups your ideas. Vote for the group with the best chance of success.

Unit 3 Reference

be going to: future

Use *be going to* to talk about something you intend or plan to do (you have already decided to do it).

A: *Are you going to see Sally this week?*

B: *I don't know. I'm going to call her this evening.*

+	I	am	going to	see Maria on Friday.
	He/She/It	is		
	We/You/They	are		
−	I	am	not going to	
	He/She/It	is		
	You/We/They	are		
?	Am	I	going to	see her?
	Is	he/she/it		
	Are	we/you/they		
	Yes, I am./No, I'm not.			

Future time expressions are often used with *be going to* (*this afternoon, tonight, tomorrow, next week,* etc.).

Defining relative clauses

Defining relative clauses give us more information about a noun.

They answer the questions: *Which person? Which thing? Which place?*

Relative clauses come immediately after the noun in the main clause.

Use *who* to talk about people, *that* to talk about things, and *where* to talk about places.

*This is **the book that** you want.*

*She's **the teacher who** lives in my building.*

*That's **the store where** I bought these shoes.*

That can be used instead of *who*.

The man that/who I work with never stops talking.

Definite plans: present continuous

Use the present continuous to talk about fixed plans. They often involve other people, and the time/place has been arranged.

When are you starting your new job?

She isn't coming to my birthday party.

+	I	am	meeting	Alan at 7 P.M.
	He/She/It	is		
	We/You/They	are		
−	I	am	not meeting	
	He/She/It	is		
	You/We/They	are		
?	Am	I	meeting	him?
	Is	he/she/it		
	Are	we/you/they		
	Yes, I am./No, I'm not.			

Be going to and the present continuous can be used to express similar ideas. Choose depending on what you mean.

I'm going to see Phil again. (You may or may not have scheduled a definite time and place.)

I'm seeing Phil tonight at the tennis club. (You have scheduled a definite time and place.)

Unit Vocabulary

Cooking and eating

eat out	cook for yourself
diet (noun)	celebrity chef
vegetarian	give (something) up

Adjectives

tasty	delicious	tasteless
awful	disgusting	mouth-watering

Sense verbs

look	feel	sound	smell	taste

UNIT 4
Survival

Warm Up

1 Pair Work Describe the photos (A–D). What words do you associate with each?

> *A woman is rock climbing. She's high up and holding onto a rock cliff.*
> *With rock climbing, I associate: scary, high, dangerous, exciting, . . .*

2 Pair Work Discuss.

1. Which activities in the photos need mental strength, physical strength, or both?
2. What are you afraid of (for example, flying, crowded places, heights, etc.)? Do you do anything to help control your fear? If yes, what?
3. What are your goals at the moment? How will you achieve them?
4. Do you enjoy challenges at work or in your free time? Why or why not?
5. Who do you rely on most in times of need? Why?

Compare people

GRAMMAR comparatives

Reading

1 Read the articles. Mark the statements below true (*T*), false (*F*), or don't know (*?*).

Tenzing Norgay and Sir Edmund Hillary

Going UP

In 1953, Sir Edmund Hillary and Tenzing Norgay climbed to the top of Mount Everest. The next challenge was to climb it without bottled oxygen. This was the goal of Austrian climbers Peter Habeler and Reinhold Messner. Doctors said they were crazy and told them not to try it. They tried it anyway. On May 8, 1978, they were about 800 meters (2,600 feet) from the top of Everest. They woke at 3 A.M. and began preparing. It took them two hours to get dressed. Every breath was precious,[1] and they used their hands to communicate. Climbing was slow. Messner thought he was going to burst like a balloon. At 8,800 meters (29,000 feet), they stopped and lay down every few steps because of the lack of oxygen. But between one and two in the afternoon they achieved their "impossible" goal. They reached the top of Mount Everest without oxygen.

Most people can hold their breath long enough to dive to the bottom of a swimming pool, but on August 17, 2002, Tanya Streeter went a lot, lot deeper. The 29-year-old held her breath for 3 minutes, 26 seconds and became the world free-diving champion. She dived 160 meters (525 feet) below the surface of the sea. During the dive her lungs shrank[2] to the size of oranges. Her heart slowed to 15 beats a minute, and she sang her national anthem in her head to control her fear. Tanya says that her mental strength is more important than her physical strength. "I am a very determined person. When I decide to do something, I do it. 'Redefine your limits' is my motto."[3]

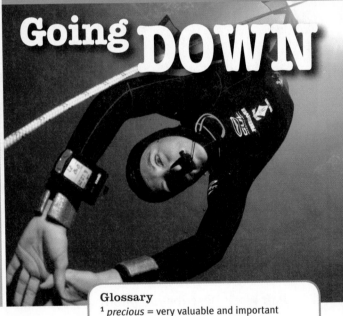

Going DOWN

Glossary
[1] *precious* = very valuable and important
[2] *to shrink* (past = *shrank*) = to get smaller
[3] *motto* = a phrase that expresses your beliefs

_____ **1.** Habeler and Messner didn't listen to doctors.

_____ **2.** It took them two hours to go 800 meters.

_____ **3.** Tanya Streeter holds the world record for holding her breath.

_____ **4.** She was afraid during her dive.

_____ **5.** She feels that being physically strong isn't the most important thing.

2 **Group Work** Discuss.

1. Would you like to try free-diving or climbing a mountain like Mount Everest? Why or why not?

2. Do you enjoy watching extreme sports? Are there any extreme sports that you have tried or would like to try?

Vocabulary | describing people

3a Replace the underlined phrases with *be* and an adjective from the box.

determined   intelligent   confident   ~~brave~~   ambitious   generous   talented   reliable

Ex: My brother <u>isn't afraid of anything</u>. He *is brave.*_____

1. My aunt <u>gives her money to others</u>. She _____
2. Ako <u>feels sure</u> that she will pass the test. She _____
3. Sarah <u>can understand things quickly</u>. She _____
4. Sandra <u>always does what she says she will do</u>. She _____
5. Joe <u>wants to be successful and powerful</u>. He _____
6. My dad <u>never lets anything stop him</u>. He _____
7. Mei <u>has a lot of natural ability</u> as a writer. She _____

b ▶1.21 Listen and check your answers.

4 **Pair Work** Talk about people you know who have each of the characteristics above.

> *My friend Luis is very generous. He always lends me money.*

Grammar | comparatives

5 Look at these sentences. Then complete the Active Grammar box.

*Habeler and Messner are **stronger than** most people.*
*Free-diving is **more dangerous than** you think.*

Active Grammar

	Adjective	Comparative
One-syllable adjectives	*long* *big*	*longer (than)* *bigger (than)*
Two-syllable adjectives	*boring*	_____
Two-syllable adjectives ending in -*y*	_____	*happier (than)*
Three-syllable adjectives	*determined*	_____
Irregular adjectives	_____ *good*	*worse (than)* _____
Modifiers	*(a little bit/much) taller than*	

See Reference page 46

6 **Pair Work** Find five differences between you and your partner. Then tell other students. Use comparatives.

> *Miyuki is louder than I am.*

Vocabulary | survival skills

1a Match a word or phrase in the box with the <u>underlined</u> words or phrases below.

> a. abilities   b. deal with   c. place to sleep   d. try very hard   e. nature

_____ 1. How long do you think you could survive in <u>the wilderness</u>?

_____ 2. What survival <u>skills</u> do you have?

_____ 3. Could you build a <u>shelter</u> in a forest?

_____ 4. Do you usually <u>push yourself</u> in difficult situations?

_____ 5. Do you <u>cope with</u> new situations well (for example, moving to a different city)?

b **Pair Work** Ask and answer the questions above.

Listening

2a **Pair Work** Look at the ad below. What do you think students will do at this school?

b ▶1.22 Listen to a talk by David Johnson, the head instructor at the Hillside Survival School. Check your answer to Exercise 2a.

3 Listen again and complete the notes below.

4 **Pair Work** Discuss. Would you like to take one of the courses at the Hillside Survival School? Why or why not?

Hillside
SURVIVAL SCHOOL
Learn to cope in the wilderness!

THE HILLSIDE SURVIVAL SCHOOL

1. David's previous work: _____
2. His "aims": help people discover nature/outdoor life; _____

Basic survival course:
3. How long? _____
4. When does it take place? _____
5. Cost? _____

Extreme survival course:
6. When does it take place? _____
7. Cost? _____

8. Minimum age: _____
9. Full payment by: _____
10. Discounts for: _____

Grammar | superlatives

5 Read this note about the course. Do the writers feel positive or negative?

Hi David,

Just a quick email to say we really enjoyed the weekend. It was one of the <u>hardest</u> things we've ever done but also one of the <u>most</u> <u>exciting</u>. Thanks a million for an experience we will never forget (even though you said our shelter was the <u>worst</u> you've ever seen)!

Best wishes,

Catherine and Wen

6 Look at the <u>underlined</u> words in Exercise 5. How do you form superlatives? Complete the Active Grammar box.

> **Active Grammar**
>
> 1. **Short adjectives (one syllable):**
>   *the* + adjective + _____
> 2. **Long adjectives (two or more syllables):**
>   *the* + _____ + adjective
> 3. **Two-syllable adjectives ending in -*y*:**
>   *the* + adjective (without -*y*) + -*iest*
> 4. **Irregular adjectives:**
>   *good* = *best*   *bad* = _____
> 5. **Before superlatives we use *the* or a possessive.**
>   *the oldest building   my best friend*

See Reference page 46

7 Write sentences using the superlative form of the adjectives.

Ex: This/comfortable chair/in the house.   <u>This is the most comfortable chair in the house.</u>

1. Everest/high/mountain/in the world. _____
2. What/good department store/in New York? _____
3. This/wet day/of the year so far. _____
4. This/boring movie/I have ever seen. _____
5. Soccer/popular sport/in Brazil. _____

Pronunciation | sentence stress

8a <u>Underline</u> the words in each sentence in Exercise 7 that would usually be stressed.

This is the most <u>comfortable</u> <u>chair</u> in the <u>house</u>.

b ▶1.23 Listen and check your answers.

Speaking

9 **Pair Work** Discuss.

1. What is the most dangerous situation you've ever been in? What happened?
2. What is the most interesting place you've been to?
3. Who is your best friend? Why is he or she your best friend?

Writing

10 Look at the thank you note in Exercise 5. Think of a real reason for a thank you note. Write the thank you note.

Reading

1a   **Pair Work** What words come to mind when you think about England and the English?

b   Read the article. Circle the topics in the box that are mentioned.

> being polite   soccer   drinking tea
> English food   libraries   driving habits
> the weather

Looking at . . . England

There are ideas about England and the English that are just not true. England does not stop for afternoon tea every day, although the English do drink a lot of the liquid (hot, with milk), and although the weather is very changeable, it doesn't rain all the time!

Also, there's a lot of good food in England. No, really! In the major cities you'll find the cuisine of almost every nationality. Indian food is a particular favorite of the English. To find classic English food, try eating in a traditional pub.

The famous English politeness is everywhere. The English use "Please," "Thank you," and "Sorry" more than most nationalities. For example, if you step on someone's foot, they'll probably say "Sorry" to you! If you make a complaint, it's also common to begin with "Sorry" as in: "I'm sorry, but this soup is cold."

You may think it strange on the London Underground that people don't talk to each other, even when crowded together in the rush hour. Silence is normal, as people read their books or newspapers. That doesn't mean English people are unfriendly. It just means you might have to get to know them first!

British English	American English
underground	subway

2   Mark the statements true (*T*) or false (*F*). Correct the false statements.

   _____ 1. The English don't like their tea to be hot.

   _____ 2. You get a lot of different types of weather in England.

   _____ 3. Indian food is very popular in England.

   _____ 4. You can find typical English food in top restaurants.

   _____ 5. The English often use "Sorry" to begin a complaint.

   _____ 6. The English like to talk to strangers on the Underground.

3   **Pair Work** Discuss. What do you think a short article about your country might mention?

Listening

4a   ▶1.24 Listen to three conversations and answer the questions.

    Conversation 1:   Where does she want to go? _____

                         What does she want the driver to do? _____

    Conversation 2:   What does the customer ask for? _____

                         What does the salesperson do? _____

    Conversation 3:   Where does the passenger want to go? _____

                         Does the driver know where it is? _____

b   **Pair Work** Look at the Audioscripts on page 75. Practice the conversations with another student.

Grammar | indirect questions

5 Look at the Active Grammar box. Complete rules 1 and 2. Then answer the following questions:

1. What happens to the verbs in indirect questions?
2. How do you make direct *Yes/No* questions indirect?

Active Grammar

Use indirect questions when you want to be polite.

Direct question	Indirect question
*How far **is** the station?*	***Do you know** how far the station **is**?*
*Where **can** I **get** a taxi?*	***Could you tell me** where I **can get** a taxi?*
*What time **does** the train **arrive**?*	***Do you know** what time the train **arrives**?*
***Is** the museum open?*	***Do you know if** the museum **is** open?*

1. Indirect questions with *be*:
   question word + *subject*

   + _____

2. Indirect questions with main verbs:
   question word +

   _____ + _____

See Reference page 46

6 Make these questions indirect. Use the words in parentheses.

Ex: How long does the trip take? (Do you know?)   *Do you know how long the trip takes?*

1. How much is that? (Could you tell me?) _____
2. Where can I get an application form? (Do you know?) _____
3. Do you have any postage stamps? (Do you know?) _____
4. How far is it to the library? (Do you know?) _____
5. Is there a post office near here? (Could you tell me?) _____
6. What time is it? (Do you know?) _____

Speaking

7a You're going to interview a classmate for a market research company. Choose a topic from the box.

free-time activities	vacations
Internet use	shopping
favorite movies	food

b **Pair Work** Look at the How To box. Then conduct your interview. When you're finished, report your findings to the class.

How To:	
Be polite in English	
Use polite words/phrases	• *Excuse me, could I ask you a few questions?* • *Could you say that again, please?*
Use indirect questions	• *Could you tell me what kinds of movies you like?*

Review

1 Complete these sentences with comparatives. Use the adjectives in the box.

> quiet   bad   exciting   ~~old~~   close   happy

Ex: She is only 23. I thought she was _older_ .

1. This restaurant is very noisy. Can we go somewhere _____?
2. That movie sounds really boring. *Murder City* sounds _____.
3. My job is pretty good. It could be a lot _____.
4. You seem _____ today—you looked sad yesterday.
5. The house was _____ to the station than I thought.

2 Complete these sentences with superlatives. Use the adjectives in the box.

> tall   friendly   expensive   fast   ~~long~~   hot

Ex: It's _the longest_ movie I've ever seen. It lasted four hours!

1. This jacket cost $850. It was _____ one in the shop!
2. August is usually _____ month in China.
3. Eduardo is _____ boy in the class. He is almost six feet tall.
4. This is _____ car I've ever had. It drives like a race car.
5. Michael is _____ man I've ever met. He loves to meet new people.

3 Add a word to each sentence to make it correct.

Ex: Can you tell me where the bathroom $\overset{is}{\underset{\wedge}{}}$?

1. You know why he isn't home yet?
2. Do you know I can pay by credit card?
3. Could you tell me I can find a gas station?
4. Could you tell whose car this is, please?
5. Do you know time the next train leaves?

4 Ask about the following things using *Do you know . . . ?* or *Could you tell me . . . ?* Then practice asking and answering with a partner.

Ex: what time/mall close? _Do you know what time the mall closes?_

1. where/find/cheap hotel? _____
2. nice restaurant/near here? _____
3. how much/taxi to the airport? _____
4. where/I/buy/map of Bangkok? _____
5. need visa/go to Ireland? _____

Communication | agree on choices with a partner

5 Which of these things can you see in the photos?

rope	shovel	blankets	chocolate	box of matches
axe	water	flashlight	pocket knife	pen and paper
tent	mirror	umbrella	first-aid kit	
radio	candles	scissors	plastic bowl	

6 ▶1.25 Listen and answer the questions.

1. Where are they talking about surviving?
   a. in a forest   b. in a desert
2. List the items they decide to take.

   _____ _____ _____

   _____ _____

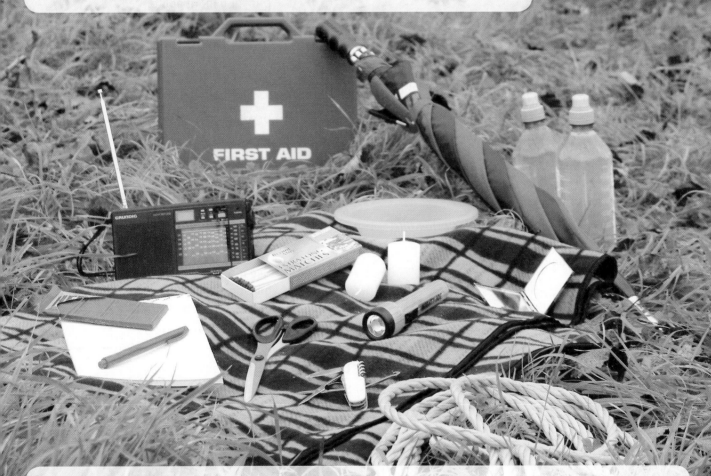

7 Read the Audioscript on page 75. What language do they use to:

1. express their opinions? _____
2. make suggestions? _____
3. make comparisons? _____

8 **Group Work** Choose one of the places from Exercise 6. Then discuss which five objects from Exercise 5 you will take to help you survive.

Unit 4 Reference

Comparatives and superlatives

One-syllable adjectives

Adjective	Comparative	Superlative	Spelling
hard	harder (than)	the hardest	ends in consonant: + -er; the -est
nice brave	nicer (than) braver (than)	the nicest the bravest	ends in -e: + -r; the -est
sad big	sadder bigger	the saddest the biggest	vowel + consonant: double consonant

*Their yard is **larger than** ours.*
*Brian is **the thinnest** boy in the class.*

Two- or more syllable adjectives

Adjective	Comparative	Superlative	Spelling
happy easy	happier (than) easier (than)	the happiest the easiest	two syllables, ends in -y: y changes to i
boring interesting	**more** boring (than) **more** interesting (than)	**the most** boring **the most** interesting	two or more syllables: no change

*This beach is **more crowded than** the other one.*
*It's **the easiest** way to do it.*
*She is **the most famous** person I know.*

Irregular adjectives

Adjective	Comparative	Superlative
bad	worse (than)	(the) worst
good	better (than)	(the) best

(not) as . . . as
Make comparisons with *(not) as . . . as.*
*Marta is **as tall as** Tom, but she **isn't as tall as** Rachel.*

Before superlatives
Use *the* or a possessive adjective.
***the** least expensive*   ***my** oldest son*

After superlatives
We usually use *in* with places and groups of people:
*What is the highest mountain **in** the world?*

Use *of* in most other cases:
*She is the smartest **of** my three sisters.*

We often use the present perfect:
*He's the most interesting person I**'ve** ever **met**.*

Indirect questions

Use indirect questions to make a question more polite.
Who are those people? →
***Could you tell me** who those people are?*
When will you arrive? →
***Do you know** when you will arrive?*

Use the word order of positive statements.
*Could you tell me what time **the store opens**?*

Drop the auxiliaries *do/does/did.*
*How much **do the tickets cost**?* →
*Do you know how much **the tickets cost**?*

Use *if* or *whether* for indirect *Yes/No* questions.
*Do you know **if/whether** Mr. Barnard is in his office?*

Unit Vocabulary

__Survival__
achieve your goal   survive in the wilderness
control your fear   cope with new situations
push yourself   physical/mental strength
skills   shelter   rely on

__Survival equipment__
axe   shovel   blankets
tent   mirror   first-aid kit
rope   scissors   box of matches
candles   flashlight   pocket knife

__Describing people__
ambitious   brave   confident   determined
generous   reliable   talented   intelligent

A

B

C

D

Warm Up

1   Look at the photos. What are the people doing? How old are they?

2   What is the typical age in your country to do the things below?

get married	have children	earn a good salary	look after your grandchildren
retire	get engaged	graduate from college	get a place of your own
get a job	leave home	learn to drive a car	

3   **Pair Work** Briefly describe your life or the life of an older person.

My grandmother was born in Monterrey in 1952. When she was a child, she moved to Mexico City. She got married in her 20s . . .

Exchange opinions with a friend

CAN DO ✓

GRAMMAR modals of obligation: *should, can, have to*

Reading

1 **Pair Work** Discuss.

1. Describe the situations in the photos. Have you ever had similar experiences?
2. What has (have) been the best year(s) of your life so far? Why?

2a Read the profile.

FROM ADOLESCENT TO ADULT

Fei is an only child and lives with her family in Shanghai. She is studying law at Jiaotong University, and she will turn 18 in a few weeks.

My goals are to get my degree, to go to Australia to study marketing, and then to come back and find a good job. China is changing, and you can earn a lot of money now in China.

When I'm earning a good salary, I'd like to do more traveling, but I have to take care of my parents, too. They're going to retire soon. They've given me a good life, and I have to do the same for them. This is the way things are in China, and it should be the same everywhere.

Usually, when you get married, you're only allowed to have one child. However, because I'm an only child, I can have two children if I marry another only child. Anyway, at the moment it's all a dream, because I'm single.

I like reading stories on the Internet. I also like reading fashion magazines like *Vogue*. I think my favorite thing is to go shopping with my friends. We can't afford to buy much, but it's fun to look in the windows and think about what we're going to buy when we have more money!

b **Pair Work** Take turns asking and answering the questions with a partner.

1. What does Fei hope to do in the future?
2. Why does she want to find a job in China after finishing school?
3. Why does she feel she should take care of her parents?
4. How many children can most couples in China have?
5. Why might Fei be able to have two children?
6. Why do Fei and her friends like to go window-shopping?

Grammar | modals of obligation: *should, can, have to*

3 Read the examples in the Active Grammar box and complete the explanations with the underlined modals.

> ### Active Grammar
>
> I **have to** take care of them.
> I **don't have to** work abroad.
>
> You **can** earn a lot of money.
> We **can't** afford to buy much.
>
> It **should** be less expensive.
> She **shouldn't** spend so much.
>
> 1. Use _____ to say something is possible.
> 2. Use _____ to say something is necessary.
> 3. Use _____ to say something is a good idea.
> 4. Use _____ to say something isn't possible.
> 5. Use _____ to say something isn't necessary.
> 6. Use _____ to say something isn't a good idea.

See Reference page 56

4 Complete these sentences with *should(n't), can('t),* or *(don't) have to.*

Ex: I <u>*have to*</u> get good grades so I can go to college.

1. You _____ spend the night at my place. We have a spare bedroom.
2. Young people in my country _____ do military service. It stopped last year.
3. I think everyone _____ vote in elections. It's our duty as citizens.
4. I think people _____ come to work in jeans. It looks bad.

Pronunciation | contractions *shouldn't* and *can't*

5 ▶1.26 Listen to these sentences. Is the final *t* of *shouldn't* and *can't* pronounced?

1. She <u>shouldn't</u> ask that.
2. I <u>can't</u> buy that.

6 **Pair Work** Take turns making sentences about your country. Use *should(n't), can('t),* or *(don't) have to.* Include your opinion.

Ex: people/vote

> *In the US, people can't vote until they're 18 years old, but they don't have to vote. I think everyone should vote.*

Listening and Speaking

7 ▶1.27 Listen to two conversations. Which two statements are they discussing?

1. Eighteen is too young to get married.
2. Teenagers only think about dating and money.
3. Young people should do military service.

8 Listen again. Circle any phrases in the How To box that you hear.

9 **Group Work** Give your opinions on the three statements in Exercise 7.

How To:	
Exchange opinions with a friend	
1. Give your opinion	*I think / I don't think . . .* *In my opinion . . .*
2. Explain why	*because . . .* *I mean . . .*
3. Ask for an opinion	*What do you think?* *Don't you think so?*
4. Agree/disagree	*You're probably right . . .* *I don't know.* *I'm not so sure . . .*

Grammar | present perfect with *for* and *since*

1 Read the website profile. Then look at the <u>underlined</u> words and answer the questions below.

American English	British English
apartment	flat
downtown	the centre of town

Ana Silva

What I'm doing now

Since I graduated from college, I've traveled a little bit and had a few different jobs, including working on a cruise ship in the Caribbean. But <u>I've worked for the same company for the last two years</u> now, and I really like it. It's a big advertising firm, and I'm an Accounts Manager.

<u>I've lived in São Paulo since 2010</u> and have a small apartment downtown that I share with Gerald, my cat!

I haven't seen anyone from school for ages, so send me a message. I'd love to hear from you!

Send an email to Ana
Send an ecard to Ana
Send a voice message to Ana

1. When did Ana start her job? _____
2. Does she still work there? _____
3. When did Ana move to São Paulo? _____

2 Complete the Active Grammar box with the past participle of the verbs in parentheses. Then complete the rules below with *for* or *since*.

1. Use _____ to refer to the start of the action.
2. Use _____ to refer to the time period of the action.

3a Read the conversation between Ana and an old friend, Martin. Complete, using *for* or *since*.

Ana: I'm so glad you emailed. It's been ages _____ (1.) I've heard from you!

Martin: I know. Well, I've been in Tokyo _____ (2.) almost two years. I'm teaching English here.

Ana: So, are you enjoying it?

Martin: Yes, it's great. Especially _____ (3.) I met this woman named Emmy. We've known each other _____ (4.) about six months now. She works in the same school as me.

Ana: Oh! That's great . . . So, when are you both coming to São Paulo?

b ▶1.28 Listen and check your answers.

Active Grammar

Remember: Form the present perfect with *have/has* + past participle

⊕ 1. *My dad has _____ (be) in the hospital **for** a week.*

⊖ 2. *We haven't _____ (see) her **since** college.*

❓ 3. *Have you _____ (live) in Paris **for** long?*

See Reference page 56 and irregular verb list on page 72

Speaking

4 Pair Work Think of three people or things that are important to you. Talk about how long you have known the people or have had the things.

> *I have known my best friend, Sam, for 15 years.*

Vocabulary | friendship

5 Match the words or phrases with the correct definitions.

_____ 1. a colleague
_____ 2. an old friend
_____ 3. get in touch
_____ 4. go out (with someone)
_____ 5. get along well (with someone)
_____ 6. lose touch

a. have a good relationship
b. someone you work with
c. have no more contact
d. start having contact
e. someone you met a long time ago
f. go on a date with someone

6 Complete Ana's message with the correct form of the words or phrases from Exercise 5.

Martin is _____ (1.) of mine. I met him in high school. We _____ (2.). In fact, we were best friends. But after school we _____ (3.), and I didn't hear from him for years. About a year ago, I got on Friends Together. Martin saw my profile and _____ (4.) again. He used to _____ (5.) with a woman named Emmy. She was his _____ (6.)—they worked at the same school. But they broke up, and Martin is coming to visit me in Brazil next week.

7 Pair Work Look at the pictures. Decide on a possible order and think of a story using the phrases from Exercise 5. Then take turns telling your stories.

> *Mateo was Karen's boyfriend in high school. She . . .*

Writing

8 Write your own profile. Use Ana's profile as a model.

Speaking

1a **Pair Work** Ask and answer the questions to complete the quiz.

LIVING LONGER
HOW MUCH DO YOU KNOW?

1 On average, which nationality lives the longest?
  a. the Japanese
  b. the Canadians
  c. the Swedish

2 What was the average lifespan 2,000 years ago?
  a. 26 years
  b. 36 years
  c. 46 years

3 By 2050, what percentage of the world's population will be 65 or older?
  a. 2% **b.** 10% **c.** 20%

4 On average, which groups of people live longer?
  a. smokers or non-smokers?
  b. single people or married people?
  c. pet owners or non-pet owners?

b ▶1.29 Listen and check the answers. Do any of them surprise you?

2 **Pair Work** Discuss. Which statement do you agree with more?
   1. How long you live depends on your lifestyle (diet, exercise, smoking, etc.).
   2. How long you live depends on your genes.

Grammar | past routines: *used to*

3 Match the person to the reason they give for living a long time.

> getting exercise   mental activity   thinking positively

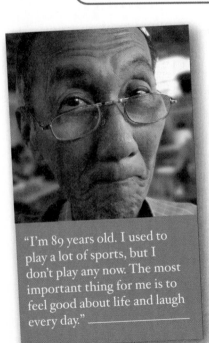

"I'm 89 years old. I used to play a lot of sports, but I don't play any now. The most important thing for me is to feel good about life and laugh every day." _____

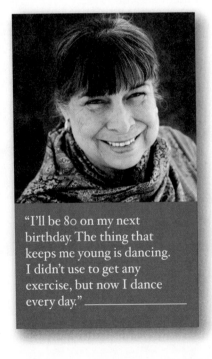

"I'll be 80 on my next birthday. The thing that keeps me young is dancing. I didn't use to get any exercise, but now I dance every day." _____

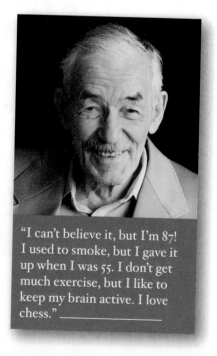

"I can't believe it, but I'm 87! I used to smoke, but I gave it up when I was 55. I don't get much exercise, but I like to keep my brain active. I love chess." _____

4 Look at the quotes in Exercise 3 and complete the Active Grammar box with *use* or *used*.

5 Complete the sentences with *used to* or *didn't use to*.

1. (have) I _____ long hair, but now it's short.

2. (be) We _____ friends, but now we're not.

3. (work) Paul _____ for me, but now he's my boss.

4. (not be) Sophia _____ into fashion, but now she is.

5. (you/play) _____ any sports in school?

6. (not like) I _____ olives, but now I do.

7. (they/live) _____ together?

<table>
<tr><td colspan="2">**Active Grammar**</td></tr>
<tr><td colspan="2">*Used to* is for habits and situations in the past that don't happen now.</td></tr>
<tr><td>➕ 1.</td><td>*I _____ to play tennis.*</td></tr>
<tr><td>➖ 2.</td><td>*She didn't _____ to play tennis.*</td></tr>
<tr><td>❓ 3.</td><td>*Did you _____ to play tennis?*</td></tr>
</table>

See Reference page 56

Pronunciation | *used to/didn't use to*

6 ▶ 1·30 Listen to the first two sentences from Exercise 5. How do you pronounce *used to* and *didn't use to*? Practice saying sentences 1–7 with the correct pronunciation.

Vocabulary | habits

7a Match a verb from A with a noun phrase from B.

A	B
_____ 1. eat	a. a heavy smoker
_____ 2. eat	b. mentally active
_____ 3. be	c. a lot of exercise
_____ 4. be	d. junk food
_____ 5. drink	e. to bed very late
_____ 6. go	f. a lot of water
_____ 7. think	g. healthy food
_____ 8. get	h. positively

b Pair Work Discuss.

1. Which of the verb phrases do you think are good habits? Which are bad?

2. Which of the things did you use to do? Which do you do now?

Speaking

8 Pair Work Tell your partner about when you were younger. Think about the topics in the box.

> *I used to want to be a pilot, but now I'm afraid of flying!*

sports	likes and dislikes
pets	hair and clothes
music	hopes and fears

Review

1 Rewrite the sentences using *should(n't), can('t),* or *(don't) have to*. With a partner, take turns reading the answers.

> **Ex:** It's a good idea to join a gym if you want to get in shape.
> _You should join a gym if you want to get in shape._

1. In the US, it is necessary to wear seatbelts.
   In the US, you _____.

2. It's possible for me to do my homework while I watch TV.
   I _____.

3. It's a good idea to get a good guidebook before you leave for Europe.
   You _____.

4. It's not necessary to drive me to the airport.
   You _____.

5. It's not a good idea to drink coffee just before you go to bed.
   You _____.

6. It's not possible for me to finish this report today.
   I _____.

2 Complete the following sentences with *for* or *since*.

> **Ex:** I've known Susie _since_ we were in elementary school.

1. She's lived in Lima _____ years!
2. We haven't had this car _____ very long.
3. They've worked there _____ 2005.
4. I've had this watch _____ last summer.

3 Rewrite each item as one sentence, using the present perfect and *for* or *since*.

> **Ex:** Sam works for our company. He joined six months ago.
> _Sam has worked for our company for six months._

1. I play the guitar. I began when I was a child. _____
2. My parents live in Boston. They moved there in April. _____
3. I have a dog. I got him two years ago. _____
4. Ten years ago they went on vacation.
   They didn't go on vacation after that. _____
5. I study English. I started three years ago. _____

4 Find the mistakes and rewrite the sentences correctly.

> **Ex:** I didn't use like my piano teacher. _I didn't use to like my piano teacher._

1. Did you use play football in school? _____
2. She didn't to get good grades. _____
3. Where you use to live? _____
4. I used like my job more than I do now. _____
5. My parents didn't use have a computer. _____

Communication | make a simple informal presentation

5 **Pair Work** Discuss. What do you know about Johnny Depp?

6a ▶1.31 Listen to a show called *Biography Break*. What is the importance of the information below?

Kentucky	20 times	age 12	*21 Jump Street*	age 16
hobbies	houses	age 20	Nicholas Cage	

b **Pair Work** Use the information in the box to take turns telling about Johnny Depp's life.

> *Johnny Depp was born in Kentucky.*

7 **Pair Work** You're going to make a short presentation about your partner. Ask your partner questions about the topics below. Take notes for your presentation.

place of birth	childhood	education	successes in life
relationships	career	hobbies	language-learning history

> *What was your childhood like?*

8 **Group Work** Make your presentation to your group or class.

> *James was born in Honolulu. His family moved to . . .*

Unit 5 Reference

should, can, have to

should, can

Form: modal verb + base form

+	I/You He/She/It We/They	should can	wait.
−	I/You He/She/It We/They	shouldn't can't	smoke.
?	Should/ Shouldn't Can/Can't	I/you/he/ she/it/we/they	go?

Use *should(n't)* when you think something is a good/bad idea.

> You **should arrive** early for a job interview.
> You **shouldn't stay** up late before an important exam.

Use *can('t)* when something is possible/impossible.

> I **can't unlock** the door with this key.

have to

Form: modal verb + base form

+	I/You/ We/They	have to	work.
	He/She/It	has to	
−	I/You/ We/They	don't have to	come.
	He/She/It	doesn't have to	
?	Do	I/you/we/they have to	leave?
	Does	he/she/it have to	

Use *have to* when something is necessary and there is no choice.

> I **have to get** up early tomorrow, because my train leaves at 7.

Use *don't have to* when something is not necessary and there is a choice.

> You **don't have to go** to the party.

Present perfect with *for* and *since*

Use the present perfect with *for* and *since* to talk about actions or states of being that started in the past and continue to now.

> I**'ve lived** in this country for six years.
> I **haven't seen** Maria since last summer.

Use *for* to give the length of the time.

> for three years, for a week, for half an hour

Use *since* to give the beginning of the time.

> since 1996, since this morning, since 10:30

used to

Form: used to + base form

+	I/You He/She We/They	used to	play the piano.	
−	I/You He/She We/They	didn't use to	do any exercise.	
?	Did	I/you he/she we/they	use to	live there?

Used to refers to regular activities and states of being in the past that don't happen now.

> Tina **used to play** the violin, but now she doesn't.
> I **didn't use to like** goat cheese, but now I love it.

Unit Vocabulary

Life activities

retire	have children
get a job	get engaged/married
graduate	get a place of your own
learn to drive	earn a good salary

Friendship

lose touch	get in touch
old friend	get along well (with someone)
colleague	go out (with someone)

Good and bad habits

get exercise	be a heavy smoker
eat junk food	be mentally active
think positively	go to bed very late
eat healthy food	

Destinations

A

B

C

D

Warm Up

1a **Pair Work** Look at the photos and the country names below. Which country do you think each picture shows? Discuss.

Spain	Italy	Brazil	France	Japan	Canada	Colombia	Germany
Korea	Peru	China	Kenya	Britain	Mexico	Australia	the United States

b Which countries have you visited? Which would you like to visit most? Why?

2a Write the nationality for each country from the box in Exercise 1.

Spain—Spanish

b ▶1·32 Underline the stressed syllable in each word. Then listen and check.

Listening

1a **Pair Work** Complete the map (1–7) with the words in the box. Which words **can't** you use?

> | Lake | Beach | Island | Desert | River |
> | Sea | Ocean | Forest | Mountain |

b ▶1.33 Listen and check your answers.

2a **Pair Work** Decide on the correct information about New Zealand.

1. The population is <u>4 million/40 million</u>.

2. The number of sheep is <u>4 million/40 million</u>.

3. The capital of New Zealand is <u>Auckland/Wellington</u>.

4. The national symbol is a <u>kiwi bird/kiwi fruit</u>.

5. You can do water sports on the <u>North Island/South Island</u>.

6. You can go skiing on the <u>North Island/South Island</u>.

b ▶1.34 Listen to the tour guide and check your answers.

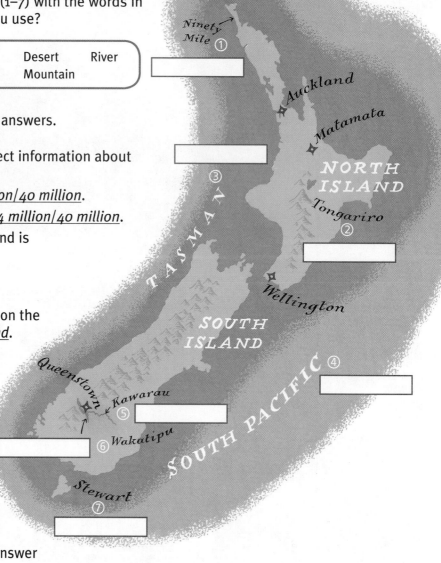

Reading

3 **Pair Work** Read the article on the next page. Then ask and answer the questions below.

1. What is the LOTR effect?

2. Why do tourists visit Matamata?

3. By what percent do experts think tourism will increase in the near future?

4. How might increased tourism hurt New Zealand?

4 **Pair Work** Find these <u>underlined</u> words and phrases in the article and say what they refer to.

> **Ex:** they (line 6) · *the islands of New Zealand*

1. it (line 13)

2. that (line 17)

3. they (line 20)

4. it (line 25)

5. these things (line 32)

For years, many people thought that New Zealand was famous for sheep, rugby, and . . . more sheep. But
5 suddenly these islands have a new image. <u>They</u> are now one of the most fashionable tourist destinations in the world. And it's all because
10 of a movie, or actually three movies. *The Lord of the Rings* series was filmed in New Zealand, and <u>it</u>'s a wonderful ad for the country. People now
15 want to visit New Zealand to see the places in the movies. Tourism in New Zealand is doing very well—<u>that</u>'s the LOTR effect. Some tourists come just to see the movie locations. For example, there's a beautiful place called Matamata just south of Auckland, and 250 tourists come
20 here every day. <u>They</u> pay 30 dollars each to see the remains of Hobbiton village from the first *The Lord of the Rings* movie.

In the two weeks after the first movie came out, travel to New Zealand increased by more than 20 percent. Experts think that the number of tourists will double in the near future, and

25 <u>it</u> won't stop there. Some people think that New Zealand will soon have over 3 million tourists a year. But there are some questions about all this success. Will tourism change the natural beauty
30 of the landscape? Will it affect the wildlife? And will tourists still want to visit New Zealand if <u>these things</u> happen?

Mount Ngauruhoe was "Mount Doom" in LOTR.

American English	British English
movie	film
ad	advert

Grammar | *will*

5   Look at the Active Grammar box and complete the examples.

6   Complete the sentences with *will* (*'ll*) or *won't* and a verb from the box.

be	pass	rain
go	see	hurt

1. I don't want to go to that beach. It _____ crowded today.
2. We don't have much money, so we _____ on vacation this year.
3. I _____ the whole country in two weeks. It's too big.
4. Don't worry about your driving test. I'm sure you _____.
5. The weather doesn't look very good. Do you think it _____?
6. Don't be scared of my dog. He _____ you.

Active Grammar

Use *will* (+ verb) to make predictions about the future.

The negative of *will* is *won't* (*will not*).

+ **1.** *The number of tourists _____ _____ (double) in the near future.*

− **2.** *It _____ _____ (not stop) there.*

? **3.** *_____ tourism _____ (change) the natural beauty of the landscape?*

See Reference page 66

Speaking

7   SPEAKING EXCHANGE Go to page 68 and answer the questions with a partner.

Give explanations for choices CAN DO ✓

GRAMMAR adverbs: *too, too much/many, enough*

Listening

1a Look at the photo and read the TV guide excerpt. What is the show *Frontier House* about?

An American frontier family in the 1800s

Frontier House

Channel 4 • 7:30 P.M.

Can modern people cope with 19th-century life?
The Clune family from California decided to find out. For six months the parents and their four children lived like Americans in the Wild West over 100 years ago.

What did they find difficult? How did the experience change them? Watch *Frontier House* and find out how modern people cope with old-fashioned life.

b **Pair Work** Try to predict what each family member will find difficult about being in *Frontier House*.

Father	
Mother	
Teenage girls	
Boys (ages nine and eleven)	

2a ▶1.35 Listen to two people talking about *Frontier House* and check if your predictions in Exercise 1b were correct.

b Listen again and circle the correct choice.
1. They lived in the style of people in about *1818/1880*.
2. The nearest store was *six/sixteen* kilometers away.
3. The father became *thinner/ill*.
4. The mother *missed/didn't miss* her make-up.
5. At first, the children *liked/didn't like* having so much to do.
6. The girls missed *shopping/TV* the most.
7. At the end of the experience, Tracy said her clothes were *more/less* important to her.

3 ▶1.36 What do you think happened when they went home? Listen and see if you were right.

4 **Group Work** Discuss.
1. Would you like to be in a TV show like *Frontier House*? Why or why not?
2. Which country would you like to live in for six months, (a) now? (b) 100 years ago? Give your reasons.

Grammar | adverbs: *too, too much/many, enough*

5a Look at the two sentences. Is the meaning the same or different?

He was *too weak*. He *wasn't strong enough*.

b Match the rules and the examples in the Active Grammar box.

Active Grammar

_____ 1. Use *too* with adjectives and adverbs.

_____ 2. Use *too much* with non-count nouns.

_____ 3. Use *too many* with count nouns.

_____ 4. Use (*not*) *enough* after adjectives and adverbs.

_____ 5. Use (*not*) *enough* before nouns.

a. *They weren't warm enough.*

b. *I'm too tired to do any more work today.*

c. *I had too much time and nothing to do.*

d. *They often didn't have enough food.*

e. *There were too many things to do.*

See Reference page 66

6 Complete these sentences using the words in parentheses and *enough*, *too*, *too much*, or *too many*.

Ex: My coat isn't ___*warm enough*___ for me. (warm)

1. I'm very tired. I went to bed _____ last night. (late)

2. I'm very busy today. I have _____ to do. (things)

3. I didn't have _____ to do my homework yesterday. (time)

4. I often spend _____ on clothes. (money)

Vocabulary | machines at home

American English	British English
stove	cooker

7 Label the pictures. Use words and phrases from the box.

> MP3 player   dishwasher   stove
> hairdryer   vacuum cleaner

_____

_____

_____

_____

Speaking

8 ▶1·37 Listen. What is the task? What do the people agree on?

9 **Pair Work** Have a discussion like the one in Exercise 8. Use the How To box to help you.

How To:

Talk about choices

1. State your choice	*I'd like to choose . . .* *I think we should take . . .*
2. Give a general reason . . .	*because . . .* *The main reason is that . . .*
3. Add a personal reason	*I couldn't live without it!* *I'm too lazy to . . .*

Reading

1 **Pair Work** What do you know about Nelson Mandela? Discuss.

> *He was in prison for a long time.*

2 Match the pictures (A–D) on the brochure with the phrases. Then read the brochure.

_____ water plants   _____ plant seeds   _____ harvest the fruit/vegetables   _____ get rid of weeds

A

B

C

D

Garden of Freedom

The charity *Seeds for Africa* has started its first prison vegetable garden at Kabwe Prison in Zambia. There are 500 prisoners at Kabwe Prison, and the prison garden will give them fresh vegetables to eat. More importantly, the prison staff hope that the garden will increase the prisoners' self-esteem.[1] The Kabwe Prison garden was inspired by Nelson Mandela, who spent 27 years in prison in South Africa. Gardening helped Mandela to increase his self-esteem.

"My garden was my way of escaping what surrounded us. I looked at all the empty space we had on the roof and how it got sun the whole day.

"I decided I'd like to start a garden, and after years of asking, I received permission.[2] I asked for 16 large oil drums and asked the staff to cut them in half for me. They then filled each half with soil and created 32 giant flowerpots.

"A garden was one of the few things in prison that I could control. It gave me the simple but important satisfaction of planting a seed, watching it grow, watering it, and then harvesting it. It was a small taste of freedom. In some ways, I saw the garden as being like my life. A leader must also look after his garden; he, too, plants seeds and then watches, cultivates,[3] and harvests the result."

(adapted from *Long Walk to Freedom* by Nelson Mandela)

To find out more about the prison garden and other projects, go to **www.seedsforafrica.org**

Glossary
[1] *self-esteem* = feeling good about yourself
[2] *receive permission* = someone in authority says you can do something
[3] *cultivate* = prepare and use land for growing plants

3 **Pair Work** Take turns asking and answering the questions.

1. Who started the garden in Kabwe prison?
2. How did gardening help Mandela?
3. What is the main reason for the garden at Kabwe prison?
4. Why did Mandela start his garden?
5. Why was the garden a "small taste of freedom"?
6. What does Mandela compare the garden to?

Grammar | uses of *like*

4a Match the questions and the answers in the Active Grammar box.

Active Grammar

_____ 1. What **do you like to** do in your free time?
_____ 2. What **would you like to** do today?
_____ 3. What **is** your garden **like**?
_____ 4. What **does** your garden **look like**?

a. *I'd like to start a garden.*
b. *I like gardening.*
c. *It's very colorful.*
d. *It's very peaceful.*

See Reference page 66

b Match the definitions with the different uses of *like*.

_____ 1. want or want to do
_____ 2. enjoy
_____ 3. appearance
_____ 4. character or characteristics

a. be like
b. like
c. look like
d. would like

Pronunciation | reductions

5 ▶1.38 Listen to sentences 1–2 in the Active Grammar box. How are *What do you* and *would you* pronounced?

6 **Pair Work** Write questions using *like, look like, would like to,* or *be like*. Then ask and answer the questions.

Ex: Do you enjoy gardening? _____*Do you like gardening?*_____

1. Tell me about your best friend. _____
2. Do you want to go out tonight? _____
3. Tell me about your best friend's appearance. _____

Writing

7 **Pair Work** What is your favorite natural place (for example, a garden, a beach, a forest)? What's it like? Make notes about this place. Then tell your partner about it.

8 Read the description in the Writing bank on page 70. Do the exercises, and then write about your favorite place.

Review

1 Complete the sentences using *'ll/won't* and a verb from the box.

| close | not/forget | have | help | pay | stay | not/walk |

Ex: It's cold in here. I think I'_ll close_____ the window.

1. **A:** What would you like?
   B: I _____ a cheese sandwich, please.

2. **A:** I promise I _____ to buy some milk.
   B: Great. Thanks!

3. **A:** I _____ to work today—it's too wet.
   B: Do you want to share a taxi?

4. **A:** Do you want to go out tonight?
   B: No, I think I _____ in.

5. **A:** Thanks for the money.
   I _____ you back tomorrow.
   B: OK. No problem. Glad to help.

6. **A:** This homework is too difficult.
   B: I _____ you.

2 Put the words in the correct order.

Ex: don't go on money to have enough vacation I
   I don't have enough money to go on vacation.

1. food to The eat too was hot _____
2. coffee isn't enough There my sugar in _____
3. far to walk too home here It's from _____
4. get She's old married not enough to _____
5. pool the There many in too people were _____
6. too chocolate eat Don't much _____

3 Look at the answers and write questions with *like*, using the cues. Then ask a partner the questions. Give your own answers.

Ex: (you/on weekends)
   A: _What do you like doing on weekends?_
   B: I like going shopping with my friends.

1. (you/for your next vacation)
   A: _____?
   B: I'd like to go to Ecuador.

2. (your street)
   A: _____?
   B: It's quiet, but there's a lot of trash.

3. (your cat)
   A: _____?
   B: She's small and completely white.

4 **Pair Work** Discuss. Match the photos with the cities. What do you know about each city?

_____ Beijing   _____ Rio de Janeiro   _____ Barcelona   _____ Mexico City   _____ Las Vegas

5 ▶1.39 Listen to two people deciding where to go on vacation. Which city do they choose? Why?

6 **Group Work** Imagine you have a one-week vacation in March.

1. First, decide which city in the photos you'd like to go to.
   Think about why you want to go there and why you don't want to go to the other cities.

	Barcelona	Mexico City	Beijing	Rio de Janeiro	Las Vegas
Daytime temperature (March)	12 °C/54 °F	17 °C/63 °F	6 °C/43 °F	26 °C/79 °F	13 °C/56 °F
One night's stay	$160	$106	$109	$192	$85
Famous for . . .	🌳 Ⓜ 〰️ 🏃	🏛️ 🛍️ 🏃 Ⓜ	🏰 🛍️ Ⓜ 🏛️	〰️ 🛍️ 🏃 🎵	🏃 🛍️ 🎵
Not famous for . . .	🏛️		〰️	Ⓜ	🏰 Ⓜ

Legend:
🌳 parks
Ⓜ art galleries/museums
〰️ beaches
🏃 nightlife
🛍️ shopping/markets
🏰 palaces and castles
☕ cafés
🎵 music
🏛️ ancient sites

2. As a group, decide on one city to visit. Try to convince other students that your choice is best. Tell them why you decided not to go to the other cities.

> Wouldn't you guys like to go to Barcelona? I hear it's one of the most interesting cities in Europe.

> Don't you think it's a little too far?

Unit 6 Reference

will: predictions

Use *will* (+ verb) to make predictions about the future.

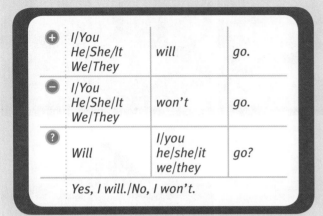

⊕	I/You He/She/It We/They	will	go.
⊖	I/You He/She/It We/They	won't	go.
❓	Will	I/you he/she/it we/they	go?
	Yes, I will./No, I won't.		

I (don't) think and *I hope* are often used with *will* when making predictions.

> **I think** the Tigers will win the Cup.
> **I hope** it'll be sunny tomorrow.

Use *I don't think he'll* . . . NOT ~~I think he won't~~ . . .

Uses of *like*

Like has different meanings, depending on the grammar of the sentence.

1. *like* = enjoy something in general
   Use *like* + gerund or infinitive.

   A: *What do you **like to do** on weekends?*
   B: *I **like going** to the mountains.*

2. *would like* = want something or want to do something
   Use *would like* + infinitive or a noun

   A: *What **would** you **like to do** this weekend?*
   B: *I**'d like to see** The Lord of the Rings.*
   C: *I**'d like a** quiet **night** at home.*

3. *be like* = asking about character or characteristics
   Don't use *like* in the answer.

   A: *What **is** your town **like**?*
   B: *It's big and very busy.*

4. *look like* = asking about appearance
   Don't use *like* in the answer.

   A: *What does your father **look like**?*
   B: *He's tall and he has black hair.*

adverbs: *too, too much/many, enough*

Use *too* or *not enough* when something is a problem.

> *His suitcase was **too heavy** to carry.*
> *He was**n't strong enough** to carry his suitcase.*

too	Use *too* with adjectives. *I went to bed **too late** last night.*
too much	Use *too much* with non-count nouns. *There's **too much noise** in here.*
too many	Use *too many* with count nouns. *There are **too many books** on that shelf.*
enough	Use *enough* after adjectives and adverbs. Use enough before nouns. *That bag isn't **big enough**.* *He didn't play **well enough**.* *Sorry, I didn't have **enough time**.*

Use *very* when something is difficult but not impossible.

> *His suitcase was **very** heavy, but he carried it.*

Unit Vocabulary

Countries and nationalities

Australia/Australian	Brazil/Brazilian
Britain/British	Canada/Canadian
China/Chinese	France/French
Germany/German	Italy/Italian
Japan/Japanese	Kenya/Kenyan
Mexico/Mexican	Spain/Spanish
the United States/American	

Geographical features

sea   beach   island   lake   mountain
river   ocean   forest   desert

Machines at homes

dishwasher   stove
MP3 player   hairdryer   vacuum cleaner

Speaking Exchange

Unit 2 | Page 22, Exercise 2a

Student A

- He sings Latin dance and pop music.
- He has released over nine albums.
- He has released Spanish, English, and bilingual albums.
- He has won one Grammy award and one Latin Grammy award.
- He has acted in one movie. He was in *Once Upon a Time in Mexico* with Salma Hayek, Antonio Banderas, and Johnny Depp.
- He has never been married, but he has dated actresses, singers, and a Russian tennis star.
- He was born in 1975 in Madrid, but he grew up in Miami.
- His father is Spanish and his mother is Filipino. His father is a very famous singer.
- His name is Enrique Iglesias.

Unit 3 | Page 31, Exercise 8

Student A

Explain these words to your partner. Your partner listens and says the word you are describing.

knife	pilot	tea	ice cream
plate	stove	salt	

Unit 1 | Page 13, Exercise 8

Student B

Unit 2 | Page 22, Exercise 2a

Student C

- He sings Latin pop music.
- He has released over ten albums.
- He has released albums mainly in Spanish.
- He has won 2 Grammy awards and 15 Latin Grammy awards.
- He has not starred in any movies, but he has been in a lot of music videos.

- He is single. He has been married once and has two children.
- He was born in 1968 in Madrid.
- His parents are Spanish. His father is a musician.
- His name is Alejandro Sanz.

Unit 6 | Page 59, Exercise 7

Discuss:

1. What are some interesting tourist attractions in your region? How would you describe them to a tourist from another country?

2. Which tourist attraction is a "must see" for a tourist?

3. What do you think the future of tourism in your region will be like? Why?

4. Work with another pair. Discuss your answers to these questions.

Unit 3 | Page 31, Exercise 8

Student B

Explain these words to your partner. Your partner listens and says the word you are describing.

sugar	pepper	soup	doctor
bowl	fridge	fork	

Unit 2 | Page 22, Exercise 2a

Student B

- He sings mostly salsa music.
- He has released over 12 albums.
- He has released both Spanish and English language albums.
- He has won 4 Grammy awards and 3 Latin Grammy awards.
- He has been in ten movies. He recently starred in a movie with his wife.
- He has been married twice. His first wife was a model and actress, and his second wife is a very famous singer and movie star.
- He was born in 1968 in New York City.
- His parents were Puerto Rican Americans.
- His name is Marc Anthony.

Writing Bank

Unit 1 | Page 13, Exercise 9

Informal email

1 Read the email below and circle the answer to these questions.

    1. What is Gaby describing?

        a. her life now

        b. her plans for the future

    2. What does Gaby ask Enrico?

        a. to come and stay

        b. to write her an email

> Informal language for greeting, for example, *Hi Enrico*; *Hello Enrico*; *Dear Enrico*

Hi Enrico,

① I've got so much to tell you. Things are different for me now. I'm living in Canada now! We're here for a year.

② James is working for a bank in Vancouver and I'm studying at the film school. We're staying in an apartment in the center of town. There are lots of things to do in the city, but every weekend we go to the country. It's really beautiful!

③ What about you? I'd love to know what you're doing these days. Send me an email soon.

Love, Gaby xxx

> Informal language for ending, for example, *Love, Gaby*; *Lots of love, Gaby*; *All the best, Gaby*

Useful Phrases

Give general news	*I have so much/a lot of news to tell you.* *We're living in Canada!*
Giving news in detail	*I'm working at a bank.* *We're studying medicine.* *I go into the city every weekend.*
Ask about your friend	*I'd love to know what you're doing.* *It would be great to hear from you.* *Please write/email me soon.*

Writing skill | paragraphs

2 Match these descriptions to paragraphs 1–3 in the email.

    ____ **a.** asking to hear about your friend's life

    ____ **b.** saying generally what you are doing

    ____ **c.** saying in detail what you are doing

Unit 3 | Page 31, Exercise 9

Informal invitation

1 Read the email and answer the questions.

    1. Why hasn't Steve written to Sophie before now?

    2. What is his main reason for writing to Sophie now?

    3. What does Steve want Sophie to do?

Hi Sophie,

Thanks a lot for your message. I'm sorry I didn't reply sooner, but I've been on vacation in Italy. I had a wonderful time and want to show you all my photos when I see you!

Anyway, I was wondering if you'd like to come to a small dinner party at my house on June 23rd at 8 P.M. Sam and Julie will be there and two other friends that you don't know. Let me know if you can come. I hope you can!

Looking forward to seeing you very soon.

Love, Steve

> **Introduction.** Say what you have done recently

> Explain reason for writing

> **Closing.** Say when you will next be in touch

(continued on next page)

Unit 3 Writing skill |
starting/ending letters

2 Mark these salutations and closings as formal (*F*) or informal (*I*).

_____ Dear Sarah,

_____ Dear Sir or Madam:

_____ Dear Mr. Davies,

_____ Yours faithfully,

_____ Love,

_____ Best wishes,

_____ Sincerely,

Unit 6 | Page 63, Exercise 7

Description

1 Read the description and answer these questions.

1. What is special about the trees in Oak Hills?

2. Why does the writer like Oak Hills when the weather is hot?

3. In which season does the writer prefer to be in the woods?

4. Does the writer live in a place that is similar to or different from Oak Hills?

Writing skill |
referencing words

2 Find these <u>underlined</u> words in the description and say what they refer to.

1. them (line 3):

2. there (line 4):

3. It (line 5):

4. it (line 6):

5. It (line 11):

6. there (line 14):

Useful Phrases

Introduction	• *Thanks a lot for your letter.* • *It was really nice to hear from you.*
Explain the reason for writing	• *The reason I'm writing is . . .* • *I was wondering if you . . .*
Conclusion	• *Write back soon and tell me your news.* • *Hope everything's OK with you.* • *Looking forward to seeing you soon.* • *Give my love to your family.*

What/Where your favorite place is

One of my favorite natural places is a nature area near where I live called Oak Hills. Many of the trees are very old—some of <u>them</u> have been <u>there</u> for hundreds of years.

5 <u>It</u> is a beautiful place to go in every season, whatever the weather. When <u>It</u>'s very hot, you can keep cool under the trees. I also like walking in the woods in the rain. My favorite time to go is fall, when the leaves are incredible colors—red,
10 orange, yellow, and gold.

Oak Hills is a very special place for me. <u>It</u> is an escape from the noisy, crowded city I live in. <u>It</u>'s beautiful and peaceful, and I always feel better when I go <u>there</u>.

Gabriela Pisani

Why you like it/what you do there

Summarize why it's special for you

Useful Phrases

Say what/where your favorite place is	• *One of my favorite natural places is . . .* • *One place that is very special to me is . . .*
Say why you like it/ what you do there	• *It's a beautiful place to go in the fall . . .* • *I like/My favorite time to go there is in the early morning/when it's snowing . . .* • *When it's very hot/cold/wet, you can . . .*
Summarize why it's special for you	• *It's an escape from the city/stress/work . . .* • *I feel happy and relaxed when I'm there.*

Pronunciation Bank

Part 1 | ▶ 2.28 English phonemes

Consonants

Symbol	Key word	Symbol	Key word
d	**d**ate	ŋ	goi**ng**
b	**b**ed	s	**s**ofa
t	**t**en	z	**z**ero
p	**p**ark	ʃ	**sh**op
k	**c**ar	ʒ	televi**si**on
g	**g**ame	h	**h**at
tʃ	**ch**ild	m	**m**enu
dʒ	**j**ob	n	**n**ear
f	**f**our	l	**l**ike
v	**v**isit	r	**r**ide
θ	**th**ree	y	**y**oung
ð	**th**is	w	**w**ife

Vowels

Symbol	Key word	Symbol	Key word
i	b**e**	ə	**a**bout
ɪ	s**i**t	eɪ	d**ay**
ɛ	r**e**d	aɪ	b**y**
æ	c**a**t	aʊ	h**ou**se
ɑ	f**a**ther	ɔɪ	b**oy**
oʊ	b**oa**t	ɑr	c**ar**
ɔ	b**ou**ght	ɔr	d**oor**
ʊ	b**oo**k	ʊr	t**our**
u	sh**oe**	ɪr	h**ere**
ʌ	b**u**t	ɛr	th**ere**
ɚ	w**or**d		

Part 2 | ▶ 2.29 Sound-spelling correspondences

Sound	Spelling	Examples
/ɪ/	i	this listen
	y	gym typical
	ui	build guitar
	e	pretty
/i/	ee	green sleep
	ie	niece believe
	ea	read teacher
	e	these complete
	ey	key money
	ei	receipt receive
	i	police
/æ/	a	can man land
/ɑ/	a	pasta
	al	calm
	ea	heart
/ʌ/	u	fun sunny husband
	o	some mother month
	ou	cousin double young
/ɔ/	ou	bought
	au	daughter taught
	al	bald small always
	aw	draw jigsaw
/aɪ/	i	like time island
	y	dry shy cycle
	ie	fries die tie
	igh	light high right
	ei	height
	ey	eyes
	uy	buy
/ɛɪ/	a	lake hate shave
	ai	wait train straight
	ay	play say stay
	ey	they obey
	ei	eight weight
	ea	break
/oʊ/	o	home phone open
	ow	show throw own
	oa	coat road coast
	ol	cold told

Part 3 | ▶ 2.30 Silent consonants

Some letters appear in words where they are not pronounced.

Letter	Silent in:	Letter	Silent in:	Letter	Silent in:
b	dou**b**t clim**b**	h	**h**our w**h**at	p	**p**sychology recei**p**t
c	s**c**issors s**c**ene	k	**k**now **k**nee	s	i**s**land ai**s**le
d	We**d**nesday san**d**wich	l	ta**l**k ca**l**m	t	lis**t**en whis**t**le
g	ou**g**ht lon**g**	n	autum**n** colum**n**	w	**w**rite ans**w**er

Irregular Verbs

Verb	Simple Past	Past Participle	Verb	Simple Past	Past Participle
be	was/were	been	leave	left	left
become	became	become	let	let	let
begin	began	begun	lose	lost	lost
break	broke	broken	make	made	made
bring	brought	brought	mean	meant	meant
build	built	built	meet	met	met
buy	bought	bought	pay	paid	paid
can	could	been able	put	put	put
catch	caught	caught	read/rid/	read/rɛd/	read/rɛd/
choose	chose	chosen	ride	rode	ridden
come	came	come	ring	rang	rung
cost	cost	cost	run	ran	run
dig	dug	dug	say	said	said
do	did	done	see	saw	seen
draw	drew	drawn	sell	sold	sold
drink	drank	drunk	send	sent	sent
drive	drove	driven	shine	shone	shone
eat	ate	eaten	show	showed	shown
fall	fell	fallen	sing	sang	sung
feed	fed	fed	sit	sat	sat
feel	felt	felt	sleep	slept	slept
find	found	found	speak	spoke	spoken
fly	flew	flown	spend	spent	spent
forget	forgot	forgotten	stand	stood	stood
get	got	gotten	steal	stole	stolen
give	gave	given	swim	swam	swum
go	went	gone/been	take	took	taken
grow	grew	grown	teach	taught	taught
have	had	had	tell	told	told
hear	heard	heard	think	thought	thought
hold	held	held	throw	threw	thrown
hurt	hurt	hurt	understand	understood	understood
keep	kept	kept	wear	wore	worn
know	knew	known	win	won	won
learn	learned	learned	write	wrote	written

Audioscript

UNIT 1 Your day

▶ 1.02 (Page 10)

M: Everybody knows that cats like sleeping . . . they spend half their lives asleep and enjoy every minute of it. Other animals have very different sleeping habits, however. These horses may not look like they are asleep. But they are! Horses only spend about three hours sleeping every day, and they do it standing up! Fish sleep for about seven hours a day, but they too have strange habits . . . they don't close their eyes to sleep.

So, what about us? Well, most people sleep for about a third of their lives. The number of hours you actually sleep, however, depends on your age. Newborn babies sleep a lot—usually about 17 hours out of every 24. That's nearly 75% of their time spent asleep! As we get older we need less sleep. Children need about eleven hours, and adults sleep for about eight hours every night. So, yes, on average you spend about 2,688 hours a year doing nothing—asleep in bed!

But you're not just asleep—you're not really doing nothing. Your body and your mind rest during this time, but a lot happens during sleep. Dreams are one way that the mind rests after a busy day. The average person spends about 20% of every night dreaming. That means you have about four or five dreams every night, or about 1,800 dreams a year.

▶ 1.05 (Page 12)

Person 1

F1: Excuse me. We're doing interviews today. Can I ask you a few questions?
F2: Sure, no problem.
F1: Are you a New Yorker, or are you visiting?
F2: I'm visiting. I'm from Brazil.
F1: And what are you doing in New York?
F2: I'm visiting my sister for a few weeks. I have summer vacation now, and I'm helping her take care of her kids. And, of course, seeing New York.
F1: And what are you doing at Tiffany's?
F2: I'm just looking. I love this store, but everything is pretty expensive, so I'm not buying anything today. But I love looking!
F1: All right. Sounds fun. Thanks very much.

Person 2

F1: Excuse me. Can I ask you a few questions?
M1: Um, yeah, OK.
F1: First, where are you from?
M1: I'm from Mexico City, Mexico.
F1: Great. And what are you doing in New York?
M1: I'm here on vacation with my girlfriend. We're not staying long—just three days.
F1: OK. And are you looking for anything special at Tiffany's?

M1: Well, yes. My girlfriend is shopping for clothes right now, and this is a secret, but I'm looking for an engagement ring for her.
F1: An engagement ring? That's great!
M1: Maybe you could help me? Could you come in and tell me which ring you like?
F1: Well, I'm sorry, but . . . Good luck with that!

Person 3

F1: Excuse me, ma'am. Can I ask you a few questions?
F3: Oh, well, yes, all right.
F1: Um, first, where are you from?
F3: I live here in New York, of course. We have a penthouse on the Upper East Side.
F1: Oh, OK. And what are you doing today?
F3: I'm shopping, my dear. Shopping is wonderful, isn't it? So much fun.
F1: And what are you shopping for at Tiffany's?
F3: Well, to tell you the truth, I'm trying to find some jewelry for a big party this weekend. Something new. A new necklace, some earrings. I'm here with a friend, and we like to go shopping for jewelry together. We'll go to Tiffany's, Harry Winston, Cartier . . . It may take a day or two to find the perfect thing.
F1: Ah, well um, I wish you the best of luck!
F3: Thank you, my dear. Same to you.

▶ 1.07 (Page 15)

M1: OK . . . I finished my wheel . . . can I tell you about it?
F1: Yes, of course. Go ahead.
M1: Well, let's start with grammar. Grammar is pretty important to me, so I've put three for that.
F1: And you're good at grammar, aren't you?
M1: Yes, I am.
F1: What about vocabulary?
M1: Well, I've put four for that because it's important to me. But I think I need to improve my vocabulary, because I'm not very good at remembering new words.
F1: OK. So . . . reading?
M1: Well, three for reading—it's pretty important to me, and I'm pretty good at reading generally, so I feel happy about that . . .
F1: Are you good at listening too?
M1: Pardon?
F1: Very funny.
M1: I'm not very good at listening, because people usually speak so fast. But I put four for that, because it's very important to me. I really need to practice more.
F1: Is speaking important to you?
M1: Yes, it's very important. I've put five for speaking and pronunciation. I need more practice, because I'm pretty good, but I'd like to be more fluent.
F1: And the last one . . . what about writing?
M1: Well, I'm good at writing, but it's not very important. I don't need to write in English much . . . just two for that . . .
F1: Two for writing . . . OK . . . Can I tell you about my wheel now?

UNIT 2 Musical tastes

▶ 1.08 (Page 18)

F: Lady Gaga's real name is Stefani Germanotta. She was born in 1986 in Yonkers, a suburb of New York City. She began learning to play the piano when she was 4, and began performing at age 14. Although her parents weren't rich, she went to a private school in New York City. As a high school student, she loved both the theater and singing. In fact, she played the lead roles in two high school musicals. Although she was a good student, she said that she "didn't fit in" and "felt like a freak" at school. At the age of 17, Stefani began studying music at New York University. A year and a half later, she left school to focus on her singing career. She began working as a waitress and performing in New York's Lower East Side clubs. She changed her name to Lady Gaga at this time, and got a job with Sony/ATV. For Sony/ATV, she wrote songs for Britney Spears and other pop singers. Then in 2008, she moved to Los Angeles and finished recording her first album. The album, *The Fame*, was a huge success all over the world.

▶ 1.10 (Page 21)

relaxed
relaxation
energetic
energy
imaginative
imagination
intelligent
intelligence

▶ 1.11 (Page 23)

M1: Have you ever won a competition?
F1: Yes, I have. I won a singing competition when I was six.
F1: Did you watch TV last night?
M1: Yes, I did. I saw a documentary about global warming.
M1: Have you ever met a famous person?
F1: No, I haven't. But I saw Madonna in concert last year!
F1: Have you ever played a musical instrument in public?
M1: Yes, I have. I was in a band when I was a teenager.

▶ 1.12 (Page 25)

F1: On *My Top Three* today, we're talking to actor Ben Parker. What are his top three records? Imagine he is alone on a desert island for ten weeks. Which music would he want? Which three pieces of music would he take with him to this desert island? Let's talk to him and find out. Hello Ben—welcome to *My Top Three*.
M1: Hello, it's great to be here.
F1: So, imagine—you're going to be alone on a desert island. You can take only three pieces of music. Which three do you want? First . . . tell us about number three . . .

▶ **1.13** (Page 25)

M1: Well, it's pretty hard to choose— but I think number three for me is "Dancing Queen" by Abba. I love it!

F1: Really!

M1: It reminds me of when I was in college. My roommate was really into Abba. This music makes me feel great. I always want to dance when I hear it!

F1: Cool! . . . so number three is Abba, what about number two?

M1: Number two is something totally different . . . it's a piece of classical music. It brings back great memories for me. I first heard it when I was about ten years old, though I didn't know anything about classical music back then. It's the fourth movement of Mahler's Symphony number five. When I first heard it, it made me cry because it was so beautiful!! I still love it.

F1: Yeah . . . So, number one . . . what's your all-time number one favorite piece of music?

M1: Well, I think my favorite song ever is "Bridge Over Troubled Water," by Simon and Garfunkel. Their voices harmonize so perfectly. Whenever I'm feeling anxious or stressed out, playing this song helps me relax. It also brings back great memories—I remember listening to this song when I was on vacation in Spain.

F1: Oh, I love that song, too! Thanks for coming in today to tell us about your top three, Ben . . .

▶ **1.14** (Page 25)

1. It reminds me of when I was in college.
2. This music makes me feel great.
3. When I first heard it, it made me cry because it was so beautiful!
4. I remember listening to this song when I was on vacation in Spain.

UNIT 3 Fine cuisine

▶ **1.15** (Page 29)

Interviewer: . . . So have you enjoyed working in a restaurant in a big hotel?

Girl: Yes, it's been great. And I've been working for a top chef. I've learned a lot, but my contract finishes at the end of this month.

Interviewer: So what are you going to do next?

Girl: Well, my dad has a friend who runs a small restaurant in the south of France. I'm going to work for him over the summer.

Interviewer: Wow . . . lucky you! Just the summer?

Girl: Yeah, but that's OK. I'm not going to stay there longer than a few months because what I really want to do is get a job in the States . . .

▶ **1.16** (Page 30)

M1: So did you do much yesterday?

F1: No, not really. I just stayed home and watched a video.

M1: Was it any good?

F1: Yeah, actually, it was great. *Big Night*—do you know it?

M1: I think I've heard of it, I'm not sure . . .

F1: Well, it's set in the US in the 1950s, and it's about two Italian brothers who live in New York. They own an Italian restaurant that isn't doing very well. The brothers want to serve the very best Italian cooking. But, the big problem is that the customers just want spaghetti and meatballs, so they don't get many customers, and they don't have much money left!

M1: OK . . .

F1: Well, next door, there's a restaurant where they serve terrible Italian food, but it's really popular. The brothers think the owner is their friend, but actually he isn't. He tells them that they should get a famous jazz musician to have dinner at their restaurant. The plan is that they will advertise that he's coming, and then lots of people will want to come to the restaurant. So they start to prepare for the "Big Night," and they spend their last money on the evening!

M1: So what happens? Is it a success, do they . . .

F1: I'm not going to tell. Why don't you watch it yourself!

M1: Oh no, you always do this, you . . .

▶ **1.19** (Page 33)

M1: So what are you doing tonight?

F1: Well, you'll never guess . . .

M1: What?

F1 : I'm going out for dinner with Carlos.

M1: Really? Who's Carlos?

F1: He's my brother's friend.

M1: Wow, that's exciting. Where are you meeting?

F1: At a French restaurant downtown.

M1: And your brother?

F1: Don't be silly, he's not coming with us! It's a blind date . . .

▶ **1.20** (Page 35)

M1: . . . Well, I'm renting this fantastic space . . . It's the first floor of this old factory. It's enormous . . . and I'm going to turn it into a really high-end restaurant. You know, there's almost nothing like that in this area. There are lots of fast-food chains selling burgers and stuff . . . but no really good restaurants.

I'd like to have about nine tables: three for two people, four for four people, and two for six people. Of course, we can always put them together for bigger groups.

I've also had a conversation with a local art gallery, and we're going to put up pictures by local artists for sale . . . with a new show every month.

I've been thinking about the menu, and I've decided that we're going to make it short and simple, but change it every couple of weeks. We're always going to have three starters, three main courses, and three desserts. In our opening weeks we're going to have as starters: goat cheese salad, tomato soup, and garlic mushrooms. For the main course: vegetarian pasta, grilled salmon and potatoes, and roast chicken and vegetables. Finally for dessert: apple pie with ice cream, chocolate cake, and cheesecake.

The food is going to be simple but delicious, and we hope to have a friendly, lively atmosphere. So, that's the plan. We're pretty excited . . .

UNIT 4 Survival

▶ **1.21** (Page 39)

1. My aunt gives her money to others. She is generous.
2. Ako feels sure that she will pass the test. She is confident.
3. Sarah can understand things quickly. She is intelligent.
4. Sandra always does what she says she will do. She is reliable.
5. Joe wants to be successful and powerful. He is ambitious.
6. My dad never lets anything stop him. He is determined.
7. Mei has a lot of natural ability as a writer. She is talented.

▶ **1.22** (Page 40)

M1: Good evening, and thank you for coming to this information session about the Hillside Survival School. My name's David Johnson. I started the school, and I'm the head teacher. I learned my survival skills while I was in the army, and since then I've used them all over the world.

Before starting the Hillside Survival School, I worked in other well-known survival schools. My real aim for this school is to help people discover nature and outdoor life, but also to learn and to have fun.

We offer a variety of courses, but our Basic Survival Course lasts a weekend and takes place throughout the year. This course teaches you the basic skills that you need to survive in the wilderness. During the course you'll have a lot of opportunities to practice these skills. The cost of the Basic Survival Course is $249 per person.

If you want an even bigger challenge, our Extreme Survival Course takes place between November and February, when the conditions are more difficult. This course also lasts for a weekend and costs $269 per person.

The Extreme Survival Course teaches you to survive in a cold and wet environment. The course offers you the chance to push yourself, both physically and mentally. No tents, no gas stoves, just you and the wilderness. You learn to find and prepare food and cook it over an open fire. You learn to build a shelter, and then you actually sleep in it. Most importantly, you learn a lot about yourself and how well you can cope with unexpected situations.

A few final practical details. You have to be at least 18 years old to enroll. The full cost of the course needs to be paid at least four weeks before the course begins. There are discounts for groups of four or more.

Well, I hope that gives you some idea of what we do. And now if there are any questions . . .

▶ **1.23** (Page 41)

1. Everest is the highest mountain in the world.
2. What is the best department store in New York?
3. This is the wettest day of the year so far.
4. This is the most boring movie I have ever seen.
5. Soccer is the most popular sport in Brazil.

▶ **1.24** (Page 42)

Conversation 1
F1: Do you go to Carson Street?
M1: Yep.
F1: How much is it?
M1: $2.00.
F1: Could you tell me when to get off?
M1: Sure, no problem.

Conversation 2
F2: Do you need any help?
F3: Yes, please. Could you tell me if you have this in a size 4?
F2: Sure. Let me go check.
F3: Thanks.

Conversation 3
M2: Hi. I need to go to 231 East Grant Street.
M3: 231 East Grant Street?
M2: Yes. Do you know where that is?
M3: Yep.

▶ **1.25** (Page 45)

F1: So . . . Which of these do you think is the most important?
M1: Well, I definitely think we should take the blankets to keep warm at night.
F1: OK . . . so you think they're more important than the pocket knife?
M1: No . . . not more important. We can have the pocket knife too, you know. We're allowed five things . . . .
F1: That's true. So what else?
M1: Well, we should take the matches so we can make a fire from all the wood you chop up with the pocket knife!
F1: Very funny. But you're right—the matches are a must. How about the tent?
M1: I'm not sure. We could make our own shelter from branches and things . . .
F1: Well, maybe you could!
M1: OK . . . we'll take the tent . . . and let's take the chocolate as number five—a little bit of luxury, OK?
F1: Perfect!

UNIT 5 Life events

▶ **1.27** (Page 49)

1
M1: . . . So then I met up with my brother and we had lunch in town.
F1: How old is your brother?
M1: He's 18.
F1: Eighteen? So young.
M1: Yes, but he's getting married in three months.
F1: You're joking. And he's only 18? Gosh, I think 18 is way too young to get married. I mean, you don't know what you want when you're 18. You haven't really experienced life. What do you think?
M1: Well, I'm not so sure . . .

2
M2: When I was your age, things were different. I had to join the military!
M3: Yes, Dad, I know.
M2: You know, in my opinion, military service is a good thing, because it teaches you how to be self-sufficient.
M3: But you can't even boil an egg!
M2: Yes, but that's . . . not important. The important thing is, young people should learn some discipline. Don't you think so?
M3: Yes, Dad, you're probably right. *[resigned then suddenly brighter]* Dad, can I borrow the car?

▶ **1.28** (Page 50)

F1: I'm so glad you emailed. It's been ages since I heard from you!
M1: I know. Well, I've been in Tokyo for almost two years. I'm teaching English there.
F1: So are you enjoying it?
M1: Yes, it's great. Especially since I met this woman named Emmy. We've known each other for about six months now. She works in the same school as me.
F1: Oh! That's great . . . So, when are you both coming to Sao Paolo?

▶ **1.29** (Page 52)

F1: Average lifespan can be very different from one country to another. The country with the longest average lifespan is Japan. Women live to 82.5 years on average, and men live to 76.2 years on average. This, of course, is much longer than the average lifespan 2,000 years ago. That was just 26 years. Now, everyone expects to have a long and happy life. By 2050, around 20% of the population will be age 65 or over.

If you would like to have a long life, there are certain things that seem to make a difference. On average, non-smokers live longer than smokers, married people live longer than single people, and pet owners live longer than non-pet owners. So the message is don't smoke, get married, and get a dog.

▶ **1.30** (Page 53)

1. I used to have long hair, but now it's short.
2. I didn't use to like olives, but now I do.

▶ **1.31** (Page 55)

M1: Welcome to Biography Break—everything you want to know about your favorite people. Today we are looking at the life of actor Johnny Depp. John Christopher Depp was born in Kentucky in 1963. Because of his father's work, his family moved over 20 times. As a child, he used to feel a lot of stress, and at the age of 12 began smoking, experimenting with drugs, and hurting himself. He also began playing the guitar around this time.

When he was 15, his parents divorced, and at age 16, he dropped out of high school. He began playing guitar for a band called The Kids, and at the age of 20 moved to Los Angeles with the band. That year he also married a make-up artist. Her ex-boyfriend was the actor Nicholas Cage, and Cage thought Johnny should try acting. Cage helped Johnny get an agent, and in 1987 Johnny got a part on the TV series *21 Jump Street*. This brought him fame as a teen idol. When the TV series finished, he starred in *Cry-Baby* and then the wildly popular *Edward Scissorhands*. Roles in the hit movies *Pirates of the Caribbean, Sweeney Todd,* and *Alice in Wonderland* followed.

Today, Johnny lives with French actress Vanessa Paradis and their two children. They have houses in France, the US, and on a private Caribbean island. Johnny's hobbies include playing the guitar, reading, painting, and collecting fine French wines.

UNIT 6 Destinations

▶ **1.33** (Page 58)

1. Ninety Mile Beach
2. Tongariro mountain
3. Tasman Sea
4. South Pacific Ocean
5. Kawarau river
6. Lake Wakatipu
7. Stewart island

▶ **1.34** (Page 58)

Tour guide: New Zealand is a surprising country with a population of 4 million people and 40 million sheep. The capital city is Wellington, but the largest city is Auckland. There are two official languages—English and Maori, and the national symbol is a small bird called a kiwi.

New Zealand's tourist industry is based on outdoor sports. Go to the beautiful beaches of North Island if you like swimming, surfing, or scuba diving. South Island is the place for you if you prefer mountain walking, skiing, or bungee jumping.

There's plenty of culture, too, with, . . .

▶ 1.35 (Page 60)

M1: . . . No, I missed it. What happened?

F1: Well, three families had to live like Wild West settlers from the 1880s. They didn't have any modern things. No TV, no phone, no shampoo, very few clothes, and the nearest store was ten miles away. One family, the Clunes from California, had a very difficult time.

M1: Why? What did they find difficult?

F1: Well, Gordon, the father, did a lot of hard physical work and he lost a lot of weight. He chopped down trees and built the house when they first got there, and basically he worked very hard all the time.

M1: What about the mother?

F1: She had a hard time, too. She couldn't stand wearing the same clothes every day, and she hated not wearing make-up. She had to cook, clean the house, wash clothes, etc., all without any machines. And they were always hungry.

M1: Did the children enjoy it?

F1: At first, they complained that there was too much to do. They had to help with the animals, cooking, chopping wood, etc. The teenage girls missed shopping and their friends, and the younger boys missed the TV and skateboarding.

M1: Did they change over the six months?

F1: Yes. They all changed. Near the end of the 6 months, Tracy, who was 15, said she didn't care about make-up and clothes . . . what is important is being with your family and friends and really getting to know them. I think they all felt the same.

M1: So what happened when they went home to their modern life?

F1: Well, back home in California . . .

▶ 1.36 (Page 60)

M1: So what happened when they went home to their modern life?

F1: Well, back in California, they loved seeing their friends again and wearing different clothes and stuff. But the children, especially the teenagers, were really bored.

M1: Bored?

F1: Yes. I think they realized that there is more to life than make-up, TV, and clothes! They really missed having all the jobs to do. They missed the fresh air and the time spent with their families.

▶ 1.37 (Page 61)

M1: OK, so we have to choose five machines we can't live without.

F1: Yup.

M1: And we're going to live in the Wild West for six months.

F1: Yes . . .

M1: As now or as a hundred years ago?

F1: As they did a hundred years ago.

M1: OK, how about I start?

F1: Go ahead.

M1: Well, we could live without a cell phone, but I'd like to choose a TV, because I couldn't live without a TV for six months!

F1: Oh, no. Not a TV! I think people watch too much TV, and anyway, we'll be too busy. I think we should take a radio.

M1: A radio? Why's that?

F1: Well, the main reason is that we can listen to music while we work—and you have to work hard in the Wild West. I always listen to the radio while I'm cleaning or cooking.

M1: OK. Good point. What else? . . . Um . . . how about a washing machine, because I'm too lazy to wash clothes by hand.

F1: Yes, I agree. OK, so that's two things. What else?

M1: I'd also like to take a . . . DVD player.

F1: You're joking, aren't you! We're not taking a TV, so how can we watch DVDs?

M1: Good point. Well . . .

▶ 1.39 (Page 65)

M1: Well, what do you think? We're going in March so we need to get the tickets soon. Where would you like to go?

F1: I think Barcelona sounds really good or maybe Beijing . . . I'm not sure. There are lots of great things to see and do in both places. What do you think?

M1: Um . . . I think Beijing is too cold for a vacation . . . I like warmer weather . . . 43° is too cold! Barcelona is a little bit warmer. Is it warm enough?

F1: Yes, I think so . . . It's warm enough for me . . .

M1: But look . . . Hotels in Barcelona are expensive . . . $160 a night.

F1: That's not too expensive. We can afford that. Let's go to Barcelona!

M1: OK . . . What's it like in Barcelona? Are there lots of interesting things to do?

F1: I'm sure there are. Let's check the guidebook.

ENGLISH in Common

3A

Workbook

Antonia Clare and JJ Wilson

Series Consultants
María Victoria Saumell and Sarah Louisa Birchley

PEARSON

Vocabulary

1a Match a verb from A with a word or phrase in B.

	A		B
_j_	1. read	**a.**	a bus
____	2. listen	**b.**	to bed late
____	3. get up	**c.**	on the phone
____	4. sleep	**d.**	early
____	5. go	**e.**	your email
____	6. talk	**f.**	nothing
____	7. watch	**g.**	in
____	8. check	**h.**	to music
____	9. do	**i.**	TV
____	10. catch	~~**j.** magazines~~

b Complete the sentences.

1. During the week, Mina gets _____ at 6:30 A.M.
2. She listens _____ music as she gets dressed.
3. On Friday night, she goes _____ bed at 11 P.M.
4. On Saturday morning, she sleeps _____ .
5. At around noon she calls her sister, and they talk _____ the phone for an hour.

c Use the phrases from Exercise 1a to complete the sentences.

Ex: You can
 read magazines
 while you are waiting for the dentist.

1. I always _____

 when I get up in the morning.

2. I _____
 _____
 with my sister every day.

3. I always _____
 _____
 in my car.

4. I usually _____
 _____ to go to work.

5. On Saturdays I don't work, so I
 _____
 _____ .

6. On Tuesdays I stay at home and
 _____
 all day.

Grammar

2   Complete the story with words from the box.

> love   like   ~~stand~~   into   hate

Arturo (26)
Mexico

I can't _____stand_____ doing nothing. I really _____ (**1.**) vacations where people lie on the beach all day—I can't understand it. I totally _____ (**2.**) exercising, so I get up early every day and run for an hour before breakfast. I'm not really _____ (**3.**) team sports like soccer. When I go on vacation, I do water sports like surfing and sailing. I _____ (**4.**) walking and biking, too!

3   Complete the dialogs using words and phrases from the box.

> ~~love~~   don't mind   am not into   am into
> like   really like   can't stand

Ex: **A:** Do you like swimming?
B: Yes, I _____*love*_____ (+++) it. I swim in the ocean every day.

1. **A:** Are you into tennis?
    B: I don't play, but I really _____ (+) watching Wimbledon.

2. **A:** Do you enjoy watching sports on TV?
    B: I _____ (+/–) it, but it's better to go to the game.

3. **A:** Do you like walking?
    B: No, I don't. But I _____ (+) biking.

4. **A:** Do you like watching boxing?
    B: No, I _____ (–––) seeing people hit each other.

5. **A:** Do you watch a lot of TV?
    B: Not really, but I _____ (++) watching movies sometimes.

6. **A:** Do you read novels?
    B: Yes, but I _____ (–) science fiction.

Reading

4a   Read the article quickly. Then write the headings in the box next to the correct time of day.

> Visit the dentist   Eat your dinner
> Think about a problem   Go to the gym

A time for everything . . .

What is the right time of day for your body to do everything?

Noon _____
Your brain works best at around midday. It's a good time to talk to your boss about a problem or do a difficult crossword.

2 P.M. _____
Do you hate going to the dentist? Make an appointment in the early afternoon. You don't feel pain so badly at this time of day.

5 P.M. _____
Are you very hungry when you finish work? This is because food tastes better in the early evening. Eating late is a bad idea. After midnight it is more difficult for our bodies to process fat, and this can give you heart problems.

8 P.M. _____
The best time to exercise is around 8 P.M. At this time our body temperature is at its maximum, so our muscles are warmer.

b   Read the article again. Mark the sentences true (*T*) or false (*F*).

_____ 1. Your brain works best in the middle of the day.

_____ 2. The best time to do a crossword is early morning.

_____ 3. It's a good idea to go to the dentist between 1 and 3 P.M.

_____ 4. Food tastes good in the early evening.

_____ 5. The best time to eat dinner is just before you go to bed.

_____ 6. It is good to exercise in the evening because your muscles are warm.

Communication

1a Read the interview. Then make notes in the chart.

Interviewer:	So, how many hours do you sleep, Liz?
Liz:	Not enough. I usually sleep about six hours on weekdays. That's why I'm always tired.
Interviewer:	And you, Paul?
Paul:	I sleep seven or eight hours on weekdays. It depends what time I go to bed.
Interviewer:	What about weekends?
Liz:	Oh, I get more sleep on weekends—about ten hours. Sometimes I don't get up until lunchtime!
Paul:	Really? I can't stay in bed that long. I usually sleep about nine hours on weekends. Sometimes I try to sleep in, but I can't.
Interviewer:	Did you know that 10 percent of the population suffer from insomnia—when you can't fall asleep. Do you ever get that?
Paul:	Yeah, sometimes. When I'm worried about work.
Interviewer:	And you, Liz?
Liz:	No. I don't usually have any problems falling asleep. Very occasionally, I can't sleep if I've drunk too much coffee.
Interviewer:	And do you use an alarm clock to wake up in the morning?
Liz:	Yes. I can't wake up without an alarm clock. In fact, I have two, because I turn the first alarm clock off and fall asleep again.
Paul:	I usually don't need an alarm clock. Sometimes I use one if I have to get up really early.

	Liz	Paul
Sleep weekdays (hours)		
Sleep weekend (hours)		
Insomnia (yes/no)		
Alarm clock (yes/no)		

b Answer the questions.

1. Who is always tired?

   _____

2. Who likes to sleep in late on Sundays?

   _____

3. Who has problems sleeping when worried?

   _____

4. What happens to Liz when she drinks a lot of coffee?

   _____

5. Why does Liz use two alarm clocks?

   _____

6. When does Paul use an alarm clock?

   _____

Vocabulary

2 Use the clues to complete the puzzle. What is the hidden word?

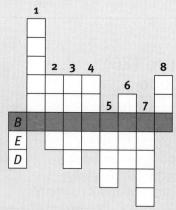

Clues

Ex: **A:** What time do you usually go to _bed_ ?

   B: At about 10:30 P.M. I usually read a book until 11 P.M.

1. Do you take a(n) _____ in the morning or the evening?

2. I _____ a book or magazine until about 11 P.M.

3. I like having a(n) _____ in the afternoon, for example, some fruit or chocolate.

4. I always _____ up very early in the morning.

5. I find it difficult to _____ asleep if I am worried about something.

6. When I am very tired I _____ a nap on the sofa.

7. Some nights I only _____ for about four hours.

8. I have to _____ up at seven o'clock on weekdays.

Grammar

3 Complete the sentences using the simple present.

Sylvie ____studies____ (study) French. She _____ (**1.** not know) what she wants to do when she _____ (**2.** finish) her degree. Sylvie _____ (**3.** live) at home with her family.

Max _____ (**4.** work) in the city. He _____ (**5.** have) a new sports car and a big house. He _____ (**6.** enjoy) going out with friends. He _____ (**7.** not smoke), and he _____ (**8.** exercise) a lot.

Albert _____ (**9.** not work) now. He's 75 years old. He usually _____ (**10.** spend) his time at home. He _____ (**11.** watch) TV and _____ (**12.** read) the newspaper. Sometimes he _____ (**13.** go) for a walk or _____ (**14.** do) some shopping. He _____ (**15.** not cook), so his daughter _____ (**16.** bring) him food to eat.

4 Change the sentences to questions. Then use the cues to write short positive (✓) or negative (✗) answers.

Ex: You live in Monaco.
  A: _Do you live in Monaco?_
(✓) B: _Yes, I do._

1. You like swimming.
  A: _____
(✓) B: _____

2. They go to bed early every night.
  A: _____
(✗) B: _____

3. She speaks Spanish.
  A: _____
(✓) B: _____

4. He goes to college.
  A: _____
(✗) B: _____

5. You have lots of homework.
  A: _____
(✗) B: _____

6. We have her telephone number.
  A: _____
(✗) B: _____

7. They remember you.
  A: _____
(✓) B: _____

8. You want to go out later.
  A: _____
(✓) B: _____

5 Look at all of the cues in parentheses. Then rewrite the sentences using the adverbs of frequency from the box and the cues.

usually	hardly ever	never
always	sometimes	often

Ex: I go out with my friends.
  (40%) _I sometimes go out with my friends._

1. I forget to take my books to class.
  (5%) _____

2. Jake is late.
  (0%) _____

3. We see Pablo and Juan after the game.
  (60%) _____

4. Do you drink coffee in the morning?
  (100%) _____

5. We visit my grandmother in Ohio.
  (40%) _____

6. It is sunny in August.
  (90%) _____

Grammar

1 Answer the questions about each picture. Write sentences.

I'm a teacher.

Ex: Does he teach? _Yes, he does._

Is he teaching now? _No, he isn't._

What is he doing? _He's painting his house._

I'm a bank manager.

1. Does he manage a bank? _____

Is he working now? _____

What is he doing? _____

We are musicians.

2. Do they play guitar? _____

Are they playing guitar now? _____

MOVIE THEATER

I'm a French student.

3. Does she study French? _____

Is she studying French now? _____

What is she doing? _____

4. Do they take the bus to work? _____

Are they taking the bus now? _____

2 Read the online profiles. Circle the correct words.

My name is Becky, and I ('m)/'m being a dancer. I _practice/am practicing_ (**1.**) for five hours every day, and I _teach/am teaching_ (**2.**) dance to a small group of children twice a week. These days, I _dance/am dancing_ (**3.**) with the National Dance Company. We _perform/are performing_ (**4.**) on Fridays at Madison Hall for the next two months. It is a great show, and I _think/am thinking_ (**5.**) I am lucky to be in it.

I'm Marcus, and I am the manager of a bank in Atlanta. I _work/am working_ (**6.**) very hard, so I _don't have/'m not having_ (**7.**) much time to see my family. We _like/are liking_ (**8.**) going on vacation whenever we can. Right now we _ski/are skiing_ (**9.**). We _stay/are staying_ (**10.**) in a small resort near Cusco, Peru, for three weeks. The weather _is/is being_ (**11.**) wonderful, and I _learn/'m learning_ (**12.**) some Spanish, too.

3 Complete the sentences using the simple present or the present continuous form of the words in parentheses.

Ex: These days I _'m learning_ (learn) to drive.

1. I _____ (not like) traveling by train.

2. Sue and Derek _____ (celebrate) their anniversary today.

3. Marta _____ (finish) school at two o'clock on Tuesdays.

4. Turn the TV off. I _____ (not watch) it.

5. Matt can't come to the phone right now. He _____ (take) a shower.

6. Sandra _____ (not work) today. She's taking her driving test.

7. Marc _____ (not think) it's a good idea to go to Spain.

8. My brother isn't working these days. He _____ (look) for a new job.

Reading

4 Complete the email with the words from the box.

> changing   doing   making   opening   planning   starting

Hi Gloria,

How are things in Spain? I hope you are _____ (**1.**) well. Here everything is _____ (**2.**). Paul and I are _____ (**3.**) a new business. It's very exciting!

We are _____ (**4.**) a restaurant called JoJo's, and we are going to serve Malaysian food.

We're opening next month, so we are really busy looking for employees and _____ (**5.**) the restaurant look nice. I hope we finish on time!

I would love to hear what you are doing. Are you still traveling a lot? When are you _____ (**6.**) to visit us again? Hope to hear from you soon.

Take care,
Jo

5a Read the article and check (✓)the best title.

_____ The Future of Shopping?

_____ The Coffee Shop

_____ 24-Hour Banking for the Future

It sells bread, milk, and cigarettes. But Shop 24 is not a good place to talk to the store owner—because there isn't one.

Shop 24 is a new idea for shopping. It's a very big vending machine, the size of a small store. It's open 24 hours a day, seven days a week. Is this the future of shopping? We decided to try it. Our shopping list: eggs, milk, bread, ham, toilet paper, fresh coffee, aspirin, vegetables, chocolate. It starts well. Shop 24 has eggs and milk. There is toilet paper, aspirin, bread, and lots of chocolate. But there isn't any ham. There are no fresh vegetables, and there is no fresh coffee.

I press the buttons to make our order. A big mechanical hand moves across the window. It picks up a box of eggs and drops it onto a shelf. The arm moves left and right collecting our order. It's fun to watch, better than normal shopping.

Then, disaster: the eggs are broken, and the door closes before I can take my items out.

We finish our shopping in a local store. It's much better than Shop 24, but it isn't open 24 hours a day. We ask the cashier about the new vending machine shop. "I think people will use it late at night. But people don't really like technology. Most people would prefer to talk to a face."

b Read the article again and answer the questions.

1. What is different about Shop 24?
   a. It has no employees.
   b. It has no customers.
   c. It sells robots.

2. What things from the list does the writer not buy from Shop 24?
   a. bread, vegetables, aspirin, fresh coffee
   b. ham, vegetables, fresh coffee
   c. bread, ham, tomatoes, coffee

3. What problems does the writer have?
   a. The eggs are old, and the door closes.
   b. The eggs are broken, and there is no milk.
   c. The eggs are broken, and she can't take her items out of the machine.

4. The writer finishes her shopping in _____.
   a. Shop 24
   b. a big supermarket
   c. a store near Shop 24

5. The cashier thinks that people will continue using real stores because _____.
   a. customers like people better than new technology
   b. Shop 24 doesn't have enough things to sell
   c. local shops will stay open for 24 hours

UNIT 2
Musical tastes

Vocabulary

1a Put the letters in the correct order.

_B_ **1.** isnreg _singer_

____ **2.** ocmreosp ____

____ **3.** dnab ____

____ **4.** rugiat ____

____ **5.** ceronct ____

b Match the pictures to the words in Exercise 1a.

c Match the sentence halves.

____ **1.** I'm really into Latin

____ **2.** I downloaded

____ **3.** I love the

____ **4.** I went to U2's

____ **5.** My favorite album is

____ **6.** I enjoy music,

a. but I can't sing.

b. last concert. It was great.

c. music these days.

d. guitar player. He's great.

e. their new song from the Internet.

f. a Bob Marley album.

Grammar

2 Complete the articles with the simple past of the verbs from the boxes.

> use   be   sing   win

ABBA
Swedish singer Agnetha Faltskog first ____ (**1.**) in public when she ____ (**2.**) five years old. Many years later, in 1974, her group, Abba, ____ (**3.**) the Eurovision song contest and became world famous. Later the musical and the movie *Mamma Mia* ____ (**4.**) their songs. Abba is still one of the world's most popular bands.

> meet   study   die   change   be

QUEEN
As a student, guitar player Brian May ____ (**5.**) astronomy. When he ____ (**6.**) Freddie Mercury, they started one of the world's most famous bands, Queen. Freddie Mercury ____ (**7.**) born in Zanzibar, and his real name was Freddie Bulsara. He ____ (**8.**) his name to Mercury when he became a singer. When Mercury ____ (**9.**) in 1991, there was a concert to celebrate his life.

> perform   become   sell   start

U2
Four Dublin schoolboys ____ (**10.**) this band in 1980 and had a hit with their first album, *Boy*. They ____ (**11.**) even more famous after they ____ (**12.**) at the Live Aid Concert in 1985. Their album *The Joshua Tree* ____ (**13.**) over 10 million copies in the US alone.

3 Write the questions for the answers, using the cues.

Ex: **A:** (go/last night?)

Where did you go last night?

   B: I went to a concert.

1. **A:** (eat/for lunch?) _____

   _____

   B: We ate spaghetti.

2. **A:** (be/this morning?) _____

   _____

   B: I was in bed.

3. **A:** (do/Saturday night?) _____

   _____

   B: I played the guitar with some friends.

4. **A:** (graduate/from high school?) _____

   _____

   B: I graduated in 2008.

5. **A:** (start/this job?) _____

   _____

   B: I started last week.

6. **A:** (instrument/play in school?) _____

   _____

   B: I played the piano.

7. **A:** (live/as a child?) _____

   _____

   B: I lived in Shanghai until I was 12.

8. **A:** (study/college?) _____

   _____

   B: I studied history.

4 Complete the sentences with the affirmative or negative simple past of the verbs in parentheses.

1. The book was boring. I _____ (like) it.
2. I _____ (have) a party to celebrate my birthday. It was great.
3. I _____ (sleep) well because there was a lot of noise.
4. She _____ (eat) a lot because she was very hungry.
5. The concert was too expensive, so they _____ (go).
6. We went to the best restaurant in Chicago. The food _____ (be) delicious.
7. There was a movie on TV last night, but we _____ (see) it.
8. She loves Colombia. She _____ (live) there for six months.
9. I was really busy yesterday, so I _____ (do) my homework.
10. I _____ (give) my sister a dress for her birthday.

5a Complete the sentences with words from the box.

after   at   ~~ago~~   as   up   of   in

a. Six weeks ___*ago*___ I sold my business for $2 million.
b. _____ the mid 1990s I graduated with a degree in music.
c. _____ a teenager I played four musical instruments.
d. _____ working for a year at my old university, I started my own business making musical instruments.
e. My name is Ibi Martins. I grew _____ in Lagos, Nigeria.
f. I finished high school in the summer _____ 1990.
g. I first became interested in music _____ the age of six.

b Put the events in order to make Ibi's life story.

___*e*___ 1.   _____ 5.

_____ 2.   _____ 6.

_____ 3.   _____ 7.

_____ 4.

LESSON 2

Vocabulary

1 Complete the brochure with the noun or adjective form of the words in parentheses.

Music Spa
Spa la la la

Are stress and lack of _____ (**1.** energetic) a problem for you? Why not use your _____ (**2.** intelligent) and take a break at Music Spa?! It's the most _____ (**3.** relaxing) spa in Cartagena!

Many of our customers have no _____ (**4.** energetic) after working hard all year. They come to Music Spa for _____ (**5.** relaxing). We offer massages and music therapy. If you prefer more _____ (**6.** energetic) activities, we have a swimming pool. Or you can use your _____ (**7.** imaginative) and take our painting classes.

Enjoy the _____ (**8.** relaxing) atmosphere at Music Spa. You will leave here full of _____ (**9.** energetic)!

Visit musicspa.com for prices, availability, and booking.

Grammar

2 Match the statements to the responses.

_____ **1.** I'm hungry.
_____ **2.** I don't like cats.
_____ **3.** I went to a movie last night.
_____ **4.** I love rock music.
_____ **5.** I didn't do any work today.
_____ **6.** I can't swim.
_____ **7.** I'm not a tourist.
_____ **8.** I was born in Brazil.
_____ **9.** I can play the piano.
_____ **10.** I wasn't here yesterday.

a. So was I.
b. I can.
c. Neither do I.
d. I was.
e. Neither did I.
f. So did I.
g. I can't.
h. I don't.
i. Neither am I.
j. So am I.

3 Complete the conversations. Use the cues to agree (✓) or disagree (✗).

A

1. A: I went swimming this morning.
   B: (✓) _____
2. A: I love the water here!
   B: (✗) _____
3. A: And I have two more weeks of vacation!
   B: (✓) _____

B

4. A: I can't stand hospitals.
   B: (✓) _____
5. A: But I like the doctors.
   B: (✓) _____
6. A: And I go home tomorrow!
   B: (✗) _____

Reading

4a Complete the stories with words from the box.

listened	really	guitar	into
instrument	bands	music	to

Pavel

Well, I'm _____ (**1.**) jazz at the moment.
I bought this album about three months ago, and
I really love it. I don't know anything about jazz,
but I'm learning! In the past I _____ (**2.**)
to a lot of rock music, which I still like. I love
_____ (**3.**) like The Rolling Stones and Led
Zeppelin. And I like hip hop, too. In fact, the only
_____ (**4.**) I don't listen to is classical. I just
think it's boring. My parents always listen to classical
music, but I just don't like it.

Helena

I grew up listening to classical music. Mainly
Beethoven, Mozart, and a lot of Italian opera, and
this is what I love listening _____ (**5.**)
in the evening. Also I'm _____ (**6.**) into
jazz music, especially singers like Louis Armstrong
and Nina Simone. I would love to sing like them
or play a(n) _____ (**7.**). I have an electric
_____ (**8.**), but I can't play it. So, yes, I love
music but not all types. I don't like rock or hip hop
music very much.

b Read Pavel's and Helena's stories again. Write ✓ for like and ✗ for don't like.

	Jazz	Rock	Hip Hop	Classical
Pavel	✓			
Helena				

Writing

5 Read Karen's webpage. Find and correct five mistakes.

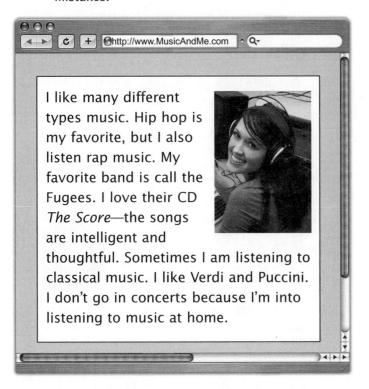

I like many different
types music. Hip hop is
my favorite, but I also
listen rap music. My
favorite band is call the
Fugees. I love their CD
The Score—the songs
are intelligent and
thoughtful. Sometimes I am listening to
classical music. I like Verdi and Puccini.
I don't go in concerts because I'm into
listening to music at home.

6 Write a short paragraph about the music that
you listen to. Include answers to the questions
in the box.

> What types(s) of music do you listen to?
> What bands or singers do you like? Why?
> Where do you listen to music?

_____
_____
_____
_____
_____
_____
_____
_____
_____
_____
_____
_____
_____
_____
_____
_____

Grammar

1   Circle the correct words.

A: Nick, tell us about your career.

B: *I've made/I was made* (**1.**) 22 albums, and *I've perform/I've performed* (**2.**) for the president many times.

A: Great!

B: And *I win/I've won* (**3.**) 18 awards.

A: How many CDs *you have sold/have you sold* (**4.**)?

B: *I've sold/I'm selling* (**5.**) about 50 million.

A: *Are you/Have you* (**6.**) ever wanted to have a different job?

B: No. I was born to be a rock star.

A: On your new album *have you change/have you changed* (**7.**) your musical style at all?

B: No, I *haven't changed/hadn't changed* (**8.**) anything. My fans love me as I am.

2   Complete the conversations with the negative present perfect of the verbs from the box.

> play   watch   taste   read   be   meet

1. A: Is this TV program good?
   B: I don't know. I _____ it.

2. A: Do you like Rome?
   B: I don't know. I _____ there.

3. A: Is the spaghetti good?
   B: I don't know. I _____ it.

4. A: Do you like the new computer game?
   B: I don't know. I _____ it.

5. A: Do you like Gabriel's new book?
   B: I don't know. I _____ it.

6. A: What do you think of Huyen's new boyfriend?
   B: I don't know. I _____ him.

3a   Complete the sentences about Beyoncé, Madonna, and Shakira. Use the present perfect or simple past of the verbs in the box.

> change   arrive   sell   act
> become   start   win

_____ **1.** She _____ in New York in 1978, with just $35 in her pocket.

_____ **2.** Her first album _____ only 1,200 copies.

_____ **3.** She _____ her image many times over the years.

_____ **4.** In 1995 she _____ a foundation called Pies Descalzos, which means "bare feet" in English. The foundation helps educate poor children.

_____ **5.** She _____ known to English speakers with the release of *Laundry Service*.

_____ **6.** In 2001, she _____ the Songwriter of the Year award.

_____ **7.** She _____ in several movies, including the movie *Austin Powers in Goldmember*.

b   Write *B*, *M*, or *S* to show who each sentence is about:

Beyoncé (B), Madonna (M), or Shakira (S)

Vocabulary

4   Complete the website profile with the simple past form of the words in the box.

> learn   give   pass   start
> travel   win   write

I was born in Korea in 1980, and I started playing the violin when I was three years old. When I was 12, I _____ (**1.**) a prize for Young Musician of the Year. I went to England to study music. I also _____ (**2.**) English. I _____ (**3.**) my music tests in 1997 and _____ (**4.**) to the United States to play with an orchestra. I _____ (**5.**) articles for the *New York Musician* magazine and _____ (**6.**) speeches at many music colleges. In 2004 I _____ (**7.**) my company, Musician Exchange. The company organizes international travel for music students.

Reading

5a Read the articles.

The Salzburg Music Festival

The Salzburg Music Festival in Austria began, in a smaller form, in 1877. Since 1945, <u>it</u>[1] has taken place every summer. For three weeks a year, Europe's best orchestras come and play the classics—Mozart, Beethoven, Strauss—at the festival. These days <u>its</u>[2] program also includes modern classical music. The beautiful 17th century square in front of Salzburg Cathedral is the perfect place for listening to the music of Europe's past and present.

B New Orleans Jazz and Heritage Festival

Jazz was born in New Orleans, and every year <u>the city</u>[3] celebrates <u>its</u>[4] birthday. The festival, which started in 1970, is full of color, art, food, and, of course, music. You can hear jazz, blues, rock, R&B, and gospel in the streets and concert halls of the city. Mahalia Jackson and Duke Ellington came to the first festival, and guest stars have included Lenny Kravitz, Van Morrison, and LL Cool J. At the first festival there were only 350 people. Half of <u>them</u>[5] were musicians. In 2010, 375,000 people came. *Life* magazine called it "the country's very best music festival."

C Glastonbury

At the first Glastonbury Festival in 1970, 2,000 people came. Now, about 170,000 people come. They dance in the rain, stay in tents, and party for three days in the English countryside. All kinds of bands play <u>there</u>[6]: U2, The Cure, Velvet Underground, and there is hip hop, pop, reggae, and classical music, too. Glastonbury is fun, but it has a serious side. The organizer and owner of the land, Michael Eavis, says, "<u>It</u>[7] is not a charity event. It's a business that gives away all the money it makes." The money goes to charities such as Oxfam and Greenpeace.

b Write the correct letter(s) (A, B, C) to answer the questions.

_____ 1. Which festivals have different types of music?

_____ 2. Which festival doesn't keep the money it makes?

_____ 3. Which festivals happen outside?

_____ 4. Which festival is over 100 years old?

_____ 5. Which festivals have changed or grown bigger?

c Look at the seven <u>underlined</u> words in the reading. What do they refer to?

1. it = _____

2. its = _____

3. the city = _____

4. its = _____

5. them = _____

6. there = _____

7. It = _____

d Change the <u>underlined</u> words to *it*, *they*, or *its*.

1. The Summer Jam Festival takes place in Cologne, Germany. <u>The Summer Jam Festival</u> is held in July every year.

2. The festival started in 1986. <u>The festival's</u> original name was "Loreley."

3. In 1986 The Wailers came to the festival. <u>The Wailers</u> sang "No Woman No Cry."

4. Many reggae bands attend. <u>The reggae bands</u> come from all over the world, including Africa and South America.

5. The festival attracts 25,000 people and is famous for <u>the festival's</u> atmosphere of peace and fun!

Vocabulary

1   Match the things in the pictures to the words below.

_____ **1.** knife   _____ **7.** oven

_____ **2.** fork   _____ **8.** chef

_____ **3.** spoon   _____ **9.** customer

_____ **4.** ice cream   _____ **10.** spaghetti

_____ **5.** bottled water   _____ **11.** meat

_____ **6.** saucepan   _____ **12.** vegetables

2   Complete the sentences.

1. I don't enjoy eating out. I prefer to stay at home and _____ _____ myself.

2. He eats hamburgers for breakfast, lunch, and dinner. The doctor told him to _____ up fast food.

3. He doesn't eat meat or fish. He's a _____.

4. There is an excellent restaurant on Avenue B. It is owned by a celebrity _____.

5. I am on a _____. I can only eat apples.

6. I want to _____ _____ tonight. Let's try the new Mongolian restaurant.

Communication

3a   Read Hannah's description of her eating habits. Then check (✓) the best summary.

> I'm a vegetarian. I gave up eating meat when I was in college, because the food was so terrible. I like eating healthy food, so I usually stay at home and cook for myself. I don't usually eat out, but there is a wonderful Korean restaurant near my house that makes very good vegetarian food, so I go there when I'm feeling lazy. I love cooking for friends, so I have dinner parties pretty often, too. I like trying to cook new dishes. I watch the cooking shows on television, where the celebrity chef has to cook a meal in just 20 minutes, and then I copy the recipes. I cook a lot of Italian food, too. It's my favorite. I'm on a diet right now, so I'm trying to cut down on pasta, but it's not easy!

_____ **1.** Hannah likes eating out in restaurants with celebrity chefs.

_____ **2.** Hannah is a vegetarian who likes eating at home.

_____ **3.** Hannah doesn't cook, so she eats a lot of fast food like pizza.

b   Read Exercise 3a again and answer the questions.

1. When did Hannah give up meat?

   _____

2. Does she usually eat out?

   _____

3. Does she like inviting people to eat at her house?

   _____

4. Who cooks when she has dinner parties?

   _____

5. Where does she get her new recipes?

   _____

6. What is her favorite type of cooking?

   _____

7. Is she eating a lot of pasta right now? Why or why not?

   _____

Grammar

4 Look at the pictures and complete the sentences using *be going to* and the verbs in parentheses.

Ex: He *isn't going to buy* (buy) a new car.

1. She _____ (leave) her job.

4. I _____ (be) a doctor.

2. We _____ (win) the World Cup.

5. He _____ (pass) the test.

3. They _____ (play) on the beach.

6. They _____ (get married).

5 Complete the sentences using *be going to* and the verbs in parentheses.

1. Pete and Sal _____ (sell) their house this summer.

2. Rob _____ (start) a new business in Australia next year.

3. _____ they _____ (finish) the work before May?

4. Jenny _____ (have) another baby in February.

5. We _____ (not have) time to see you before we leave.

6. _____ you _____ (visit) the pyramids when you go to Egypt?

7. We _____ (try) that new Chinese restaurant this evening.

8. I _____ (not be) at the party on Saturday.

6 Find and correct the nine mistakes.

1. A: What are you going on your vacation?

   B: We're going visit my cousins in Mexico.

2. A: What your plans for next year?

   B: I going to look for a job because I need to earn some money.

3. A: What you going to do next weekend?

   B: I'm going stay at home at Saturday to study.

4. A: What are you plans after graduation?

   B: I to go to work abroad.

LESSON 2

Reading

1a Read the movie reviews. Which is positive and which is negative?

Positive: _____ Negative: _____

FAST FOOD IN A FAST WORLD

This film is set in Canada. The story is about Julie (Jane Wild), a waitress who goes on a date with a doctor named Carl (Tom Payne). She doesn't know that Carl already has an ex-wife and some kids. He doesn't know that she has an identical twin.

Fast Food in a Fast World doesn't have an exciting story or fast food. And it doesn't have any laughs. When Julie receives lots of money from a relative who dies, it is the happy ending to the story. But, unfortunately, this is not a very good movie.

My Big Fat Greek Wedding

This is the story of 30-year-old Toula (Nia Vardalos), who falls in love with Ian (John Corbett). The only problem is that he's not Greek. According to the film, Greek women should get married (to Greek men), have lots of babies, and feed lots of people. Will her family be happy if she marries a non-Greek? Maybe not. Will they accept her decision when they see that she is happy? The answer is yes, and the rest of the film is about the wedding.

It's not a great story, but the film is very funny. The first hour, when we learn about the relationships in a Greek family, has some very good humor.

My Big Fat Greek Wedding shows us a traditional wedding and at the same time talks about accepting people who are different from us.

b Mark the sentences true (*T*) or false (*F*).

_____ 1. *Fast Food in a Fast World* is about Canadian doctors.

_____ 2. The story ends happily when Julie gets some unexpected money.

_____ 3. *My Big Fat Greek Wedding* is about a young Greek couple who get married.

_____ 4. It is a funny film that talks about Greek family relationships.

c Find the words in the reviews that have these meanings:

1. _____ = go to a restaurant, movie, etc., with someone you like in a romantic way

2. _____ = informal word for *children*

3. _____ = British word for *movie*

4. _____ = to say yes to something/ to agree

Grammar

2 Put the words in order to make sentences.

1. use/It's/bottles./for opening/that/you/something

   _____

2. that/thing/you/It's/to/the/dry/use/your hair

   _____

3. stuff/bread./can put/It's/you/the/on/that

   _____

4. the/met/the people/They're/we/at/party.

   _____

5. the/where/Vancouver/city/was/born./I/is

   _____

6. that/restaurant/best/like/I/Grazie./the/is

   _____

3a Complete the clues with *who, that,* or *where*.

Clues

Down

1. It's a food _____ is very cold.
2. It's someone _____ eats in a restaurant.
3. They are the instructions _____ you use for cooking a particular dish.
6. They are things _____ you use for cutting.
7. It's the meal _____ you eat in the middle of the day.

Across

4. He's the person _____ serves your food.
5. It's a place _____ you can buy fresh fruit and vegetables.
8. It's the room _____ a chef works.
9. She's the person _____ cooks your meal.

b Use the clues to complete the crossword puzzle.

4 Match the sentence halves. Then write sentences with *who, that,* or *where* on a piece of notepaper.

_e_ 1. A builder is someone
___ 2. An oven is a machine
___ 3. An airport is a place
___ 4. A pilot is someone
___ 5. A pencil is something
___ 6. An author is someone
___ 7. A movie theater is a place
___ 8. A menu is something

a. flies planes.
b. writes books.
c. lists food served in a restaurant.
d. you use for writing or drawing.
e. builds houses.
f. makes food hot.
g. people catch planes.
h. you can watch movies.

Ex:
> 1. A builder is someone who builds houses.

Writing

5 There are 20 mistakes in spelling, punctuation, and capitalization in this letter. Find and correct them.

Dear Keiko,

  Thanks for your letter. Im sorry I didn't reply sooner, but I only recieved your letter this morning. I have been away on vacation whit my sister, and I only came home yesterday. We went camping in Canada, wich was beautifull exept for the wether. It rained nearly every day!

  Its very kind of you to invite me to stay. I would love to come to japan, and it would be great to see you again. We haven't seen each other for nearly tow years now—I can't belief it. I could come for the last weekend in september (27/28). I am finishing my job, so I will have a few days free. Would that be OK with you?

  Anyway, I hop you well, and I am looking foward to hearing your news. How is your class going Are you still planing to open a flower busness when you finnish?

Talk to you soon.

Paola

Vocabulary

1 Replace the underlined words with the correct word or phrase.

1. Did you make this chocolate cake? It's <u>expensive</u>!

   _____

2. I can't eat snails. I think they are <u>delicious</u>!

   _____

3. This fruit salad <u>feels</u> mouth-watering. Would you like some?

   _____

4. I think the soup needs salt or something. It's a little <u>tasty</u>.

   _____

5. That meat looks awful. I think it's <u>young</u>.

   _____

6. This magazine is full of <u>soft</u> recipes.

   _____

2 Complete the article with the words from the box.

> appearance   dishes   rating
> ingredients   location   texture

Great Ideas for Restaurant Owners

The area
The most important thing is to find a good _____ (**1.**) for your restaurant. Why get a good _____ (**2.**) from food critics if there are no customers in your area?

The chef
Find an experienced chef, but make sure you try his or her cooking first. The food has to have a good _____ (**3.**) and _____ (**4.**), and has to taste delicious, too!
Ask the chef to cook you a few different _____ (**5.**) from the menu so that you can be sure the chef can cook the recipes you want.

The food
You need to know where to buy the freshest _____ (**6.**) for your menu. Your chef may know, so ask him or her first.

3 Match a verb from A with an adjective from B to complete the sentences.

A	B
looks feels smells tastes sounds	delicious expensive old soft awful

1. Not again! That music _____ _____ .

2. I don't think it's any good. It _____ _____ .

3. This sweater _____ so _____ .

4. This meal _____ _____ .

5. That dress _____ _____ .

Grammar

4 Complete the conversations with the present continuous. Use the words in parentheses. Use contracted forms where possible.

1. A: What _____ (you/do) this evening?
   B: I _____ (stay) at home and _____ (watch) television.

2. A: _____ (you/cook) dinner later?
   B: No. We _____ (order) a pizza.

3. A: _____ (you/do) anything this afternoon?
   B: I don't know. I _____ (not play) tennis with Pete because _____ (rain).

4. A: How _____ (you/get) home from the meeting?
   B: I _____ (not drive). I _____ (take) the six o'clock train.

5. A: _____ (you/come) to the soccer match on Saturday?
   B: Yes. We _____ (bring) a friend, too.

6. A: _____ (you/come) to the office on Monday?
   B: No. I _____ (not work) next week.

5 Complete the sentences with the present continuous form of the verbs from the box.

meet	move	leave	finish	go
take	work	have	play	visit

1. We _____ sailing this weekend on Jack's new boat.

2. They _____ for Brazil on Friday morning.

3. I _____ the Natural History Museum this afternoon.

4. He _____ the bank manager tomorrow morning.

5. _____ you _____ soccer on Saturday?

6. We _____ not _____ this month. Our new house isn't ready.

7. She _____ a baby soon.

8. _____ they _____ a train to New York?

9. We _____ on this project for the next two weeks.

10. He _____ the painting tomorrow.

6a Read Jim's phone conversations. Number the lines of the conversations in the correct order.

Conversation 1
_____ Hi, Jim.
_____ Thanks, Jim.
_____ Not really. I'm staying home to study.
__1__ Hello, Sal. It's Jim.
_____ Sure. I'll call you again next week. Good luck with your studies!
_____ Oh, I'm sorry, but I don't like going out when I have to study. Maybe another time?
_____ Are you doing anything this weekend?
_____ Oh. Well, why don't we go out Saturday night? There's a new restaurant opening on the river . . .

Conversation 2
_____ What are you doing on Saturday night?
_____ Hello, Bella? It's Jim.
_____ Perfect! I can meet you at 7 P.M.
_____ Nothing. Why?
_____ Great!
_____ Well, would you like to go out for dinner?
_____ Hi, Jim.
_____ Great idea! Oh, wait a minute. Saturday? No, I just remembered. I'm going to a concert on Saturday. Diane bought tickets to see The White Stripes. How about Sunday night?

b Read the conversations again. Write notes in the chart.

Sal	Bella
Plans for Saturday: *staying at home*	Plans for Saturday:
Reason:	Reason:

c Complete the sentences about Sal's and Bella's plans for the weekend.
1. Sal _is staying home to study_____.
2. On Saturday, Bella _____.
3. On Sunday, Bella _____.

Simple present and present continuous

1 Circle the correct words.

1. *Are you leaving/Do you leave* now?
2. Sam *doesn't usually wear/isn't usually wearing* jeans.
3. I *am never watching/never watch* TV.
4. Who *does James talk/is James talking* to?
5. *Do you know/Are you knowing* my wife, Samira?
6. She *is sometimes going/sometimes goes* out.
7. A: Can I help you?
   B: I *look/am looking* for this dress in a size 12.
8. The manager *often has lunch/is often having lunch* in his office.
9. A: What *are you doing/do you do*?
   B: I'm waiting for the train.
10. It *doesn't rain/isn't raining* now.

2 Use the cues to write questions. Then match the questions to the answers below.

___e___ 1. What/you/do?

_____ 2. Where/you/go?

_____ 3. What/she/eat?

_____ 4. What time/you/get home?

_____ 5. you/go/the store?

_____ 6. What/Paul/do?

_____ 7. How/get/to work?

_____ 8. Jayne/have/a car?

a. Yes. Do you want me to buy something?
b. No, she doesn't.
c. I walk.
d. To the dentist. I have an appointment.
e. I'm a teacher.
f. Usually at about 7 P.M.
g. He's playing tennis.
h. Vegetable soup with pasta.

Simple past and present perfect

3 Circle the correct words.

Goddesses

The Goddesses are a new girl band from Dublin. They *started/have started* (**1.**) playing in 2002 and *have made/made* (**2.**) fourteen albums. Their first album *sold/has sold* (**3.**) 50,000 copies in the first two months. They *have won/won* (**4.**) the Irish Music Awards twice and *have toured/toured* (**5.**) around Europe and America. Why *have they been/were they* (**6.**) so successful?

Amy and Sam, the lead singers, are sisters. "We *have always loved/always loved* (**7.**) singing. When we were in elementary school we *started/have started* (**8.**) a band with some friends and *sang/have sung* (**9.**) in a concert at the end of the year. It *was/has been* (**10.**) a big success. Since that day we *have always been/were always* (**11.**) very lucky."

4 Complete the conversations using the simple past or the present perfect form of the verb in parentheses.

1. A: _____ you ever _____ (go) to Brazil?
   B: Yes. I _____ (go) to Carnival in Rio last year.

2. A: I _____ (live) in Hong Kong for five years now.
   B: Why _____ you _____ (move) there?

3. A: _____ you _____ (visit) any interesting sights in Beijing when you were there?
   B: No. We _____ (not have) enough time.

4. A: _____ you ever _____ (see) any famous bands in concert?
   B: I _____ (see) Pearl Jam when I was a teenager.

Be going to and present continuous for definite plans

5 Correct the mistake in each sentence.

1. We leaving on Friday at 2 P.M.
2. Are you go to see Han this weekend?
3. I'm have lunch with my mother tomorrow.
4. We is meeting in Central Park.
5. Do they coming to the party tonight?
6. I amn't flying to Hong Kong.
7. He is to go to buy a new computer later.
8. We aren't going drive through the mountains.
9. Is Mark to playing soccer on Saturday?
10. Maria isn't comes to the restaurant.

Defining relative clauses

6 Complete the sentences using *that, who,* or *where.*

1. It's the place _____ I like to sit and read.
2. She's someone _____ I can talk to.
3. It's the thing _____ you use for cutting food.
4. That's the movie _____ I told you about.
5. This is the office _____ we can work.
6. That is the theater _____ I saw my first concert.
7. He's the man _____ told me about the job.
8. That is the restaurant _____ we met.

7 Rewrite the sentences using the relative clauses from the box.

> who has his own software company
> that you lost
> that has rooms for $100
> where we had our first meal together
> who offered me her seat on the bus
> ~~that you gave me~~

1. I can't find that bag *that you gave me.*
2. Are these the keys _____?
3. Do you remember the restaurant _____ _____?
4. Do you know the name of that hotel _____ _____?

5. That's the woman _____ _____.
6. My sister introduced me to a man _____ _____.

Vocabulary

8 Put the words from the box in the correct groups.

> fall asleep   classical   lamb
> get up early   energetic   onion
> bottled water   intelligent   pizza
> play the violin   vegetable   singer
> read a magazine   chocolate   concert

1. food: _____ _____
2. daily routines: _____ _____
3. music: _____ _____
4. adjectives: _____ _____

9 Complete the sentences using the words from the box.

> relaxed   into   tasty   test   checked
> download   nap   picnic   cook   started

1. Do you _____ for yourself or do you prefer to eat out?
2. I'm very tired. I think I'll take a(n) _____ this afternoon.
3. It's a very sunny day. Why don't we buy some food and have a(n) _____ in the park?
4. I'm really _____ jazz right now.
5. I don't buy CDs anymore. I usually _____ music from the Internet.
6. I took a hot bath and got a massage, and I felt very _____.
7. Tim is working very hard because he just _____ his own company.
8. This is a very _____ recipe. I've never cooked apples like this before.
9. I've been away, so I haven't _____ my email for a few days.
10. I passed a difficult _____.

Survival

Vocabulary

1 Put the <u>underlined</u> letters in order to complete the sentences.

1. I held my <u>btrahe</u> when I was under the water. _____

2. I don't have the <u>ahpcsiyl eshrtgtn</u> to swim for two hours a day. _____

3. You need <u>netlam</u> strength to cope with bad news. _____

4. I <u>tcdenrlloo</u> my fear under water, but it was difficult. _____

5. We <u>lyre</u> on our co-workers because we can't work alone. _____

6. I haven't <u>cahevide</u> my goals. I want to travel the world. _____

7. The biggest <u>ehlgclena</u> in sports is winning an Olympic medal. _____

Grammar

2a Read the ads. Answer the questions.

ABT EXTREME SPORTS VACATIONS
Kayaking, mountain climbing, base jumping, and free-diving

ACCOMMODATIONS:
4-star hotel, all meals provided

YOU NEED TO BE:
over 16, a strong swimmer, very fit

COST:
$500 for one week or $1,500 for one month

Knockout Vacations
Try 15 extreme sports! Minimum age is 18. No experience necessary. Beginners welcome. Non-stop fun and games!
Accommodation: simple apartments for 6 people. Price: $349 per person. All vacations last 7 days. For a knockout vacation you will never forget!

1. What are both ads about? _____

2. What kinds of people will respond to these ads? _____

b Complete the sentences using the words in parentheses.

1. The courses at ABT are _____ _____ (expensive) the courses at Knockout.

2. ABT has _____ (good) accommodations _____ Knockout.

3. Knockout sounds _____ _____ _____ (enjoyable) ABT.

4. Knockout seems _____ _____ (friendly) ABT.

5. You can take _____ (long) classes at ABT.

6. Knockout has a(n) _____ (great) variety _____ ABT.

7. ABT welcomes people who are _____ _____ (young) 18.

3 Correct the sentences.

1. It was much more bad this morning. It rained for hours.

2. It was most interesting than his last one, and I liked all of the actors.

3. This one is more cheap than the other place, and breakfast is included.

4. It's gooder than my last one because I have a nice manager.

4 Do the pairs of sentences have the same (S) or a different (D) meaning?

_____ 1. a. Keisuke was younger than Joe.
       b. Joe wasn't older than Keisuke.

_____ 2. a. The Hilton is more expensive than the Marriott.
       b. The Marriott is cheaper than the Hilton.

_____ 3. a. I can run faster than my brother.
       b. My brother runs slower than me.

_____ 4. a. The first exam was easier than the second.
       b. The second exam was more difficult than the first.

_____ 5. a. My French is worse than my Spanish.
       b. I speak better French than Spanish.

5 Complete the sentences so that they mean the same. Use the cues.

1. The Atlantic Ocean is 82.4 million square kilometers (31.8 million square miles). The Pacific is 165.2 million square kilometers (63.8 million square miles).
   (large) The Pacific is
   _____ the Atlantic.

2. Mountain climbing is difficult. Without oxygen it is very difficult.
   (difficult) Mountain climbing without oxygen is
   _____ mountain climbing with oxygen.

3. Physical strength is important for divers. Mental strength is very important.
   (important) Mental strength is
   _____ physical strength for divers.

4. Temba Tsheri climbed Mount Everest when he was 15. Sherman Bull May climbed Mount Everest when he was 64.
   (young) Temba Tsheri was
   _____ Sherman Bull May when he climbed Mount Everest.

Vocabulary

6 Use the clues to complete the puzzle. What is the hidden word?

1	G	E	N	E	R	O	U	S		
2										
3										
4										
5										
6										
7						E				

Clues

1. She gives lots of presents to her friends. She's really _____.
2. No one can stop him when he wants something. He's really _____.
3. She solves problems and understands things easily. She's _____.
4. She is sure that she is good enough. She's very _____.
5. He wants to be manager of this company by the time he's 30. He's _____.

6. She wasn't frightened when she saw the lion. She's very _____.
7. He's good at basketball, he's a great artist, and he speaks five languages. He's very _____.

Reading

7 Read the story. Mark the sentences true (*T*) or false (*F*).

Running Man

His friends call him Running Man. British runner Robert Garside ran around the world on an incredible six-year journey from 1997 to 2009. In 2007 he was named by the Guinness Book of World Records as the first person to run across six continents.

His journey had problems. In Russia, someone tried to shoot him. In China, police put him in prison for five days. In Pakistan, he was robbed and left with just his clothes and passport. When he called his girlfriend to tell her, she ended their relationship! In Australia, police stopped Robert when they found him running in 55° (131° Fahrenheit) heat.

Robert traveled lightly. He carried a Walkman with cassettes of Pavarotti and Beethoven, a letter from Nelson Mandela, and a camera. He ran for eight hours each day, through 29 countries for a total of 56,000 kilometers (35,000 miles). His friends thought he was crazy. "I just wanted to do something different. I'm a very normal person," he said.

_____ 1. Robert Garside has run across six continents.
_____ 2. Garside robbed someone in China.
_____ 3. He broke up with his girlfriend during his journey.
_____ 4. He went to prison in Australia.
_____ 5. He carried a photo of Nelson Mandela.
_____ 6. He listened to music.
_____ 7. He ran about 35,000 miles.
_____ 8. He thinks he is a normal person.

Vocabulary

1 Match the sentence halves.

_____ 1. I'm good at coping   **a.** challenges in my job.

_____ 2. I learned survival   **b.** with problems at work.

_____ 3. There are many big   **c.** I love the wilderness.

_____ 4. I like to push   **d.** a shelter at survival school.

_____ 5. I live in a city, but   **e.** skills in the army.

_____ 6. We learned to build   **f.** myself to the limit.

2 Complete the message with the words from the box.

> skills   challenges   myself   wilderness   cope   shelter

Hello,

My name is Billy Bones. I have lived on a desert island for about two years. Living here is full of big _____ (1.). I learned survival _____ (2.) on this island, and I built a _____ (3.) because it rains a lot. But I'm happy now. I can _____ (4.) with any problem, and I love to push _____ (5.). So why am I writing this letter? Because surviving in the _____ (6.) can be lonely, so I'm looking for a pen pal. Please write soon. *BB*

Grammar

3 Use the cues to write sentences.

> **Ex:** seen/beautiful countries
>
> *I've seen some beautiful countries, but this is the most beautiful.*

1. watch/boring movies

_____

2. have/bad days

_____

3. play in/great games

_____

4. live in/quiet places

_____

5. stay in/expensive hotels

_____

6. have/long conversations

_____

7. learn/important lessons

_____

8. have/crazy moments

_____

4 Read the review and make superlatives from the words in parentheses.

SURVIVOR!

It's like the TV show *Big Brother*, but on an island! Who will survive this time? Here are the four remaining contestants.

Mike is, physically, _the strongest_ (1. strong) contestant. He loves nature, and he likes to push himself to the limit. He isn't _____ (2. intelligent) contestant.

Clara is from Santos, Brazil. She loves water, and she is _____ (3. good) swimmer in the group. She is _____ (4. small) contestant, but she has many survival skills.

Chin-Hwa likes challenges. He was in the Korean army for five years. He says it was _____ (5. hard) time of his life, but he enjoyed it. Chin-Hwa is _____ (6. popular) contestant because he has a good sense of humor.

Virginia is _____ (7. tall) contestant. She played basketball for the US women's team. Now she works in a survival school. She is _____ (8. fit) person in the group.

5 Write sentences with the same meaning. Use the cues.

1. No runner is faster than Lewis.
   (the) Lewis is _____ runner in the world.
2. I have never eaten better food!
   (ever) This is the _____ _____ eaten!

3. No other country in Central America has more tourists than Costa Rica.
   (popular) Costa Rica is _____ tourist destination in Central America.
4. I've never stayed in a house this beautiful.
   (have) This is the _____ _____ ever stayed in.
5. The other theaters in town are bigger than this one.
   (theater) This is _____ town.
6. He weighs 100 kilograms (220 pounds). The other boys are not so heavy.
   (heavy) He is _____ boy in the group.
7. None of the other songs on the album are as good as this.
   (the) This is _____ song on the album.

Writing

6 Choose the correct words to complete the letter.

> Dear Josie,
> A _____ (1.) thank-you for last Saturday. I _____ (2.) a really good time, and the barbecue was really _____ (3.). The fish was the most delicious I've _____ (4.) tasted! Also, thank you for _____ (5.) me to cook shrimp! We _____ (6.) love to do it again, but next time at our place!
> _____ (7.) wishes,
> Marcin

1.	small	big	great	real
2.	enjoyed	spent	had	was
3.	funny	enjoyable	fun	time
4.	ever	always	been	never
5.	help	teaching	making	show
6.	would	will	do	can
7.	Love	Kind	Nice	Best

Grammar

1 Put the words in the correct order to complete the questions.

1. what/is/it/time

   Could you tell me _____ ?

2. can/an/Internet/café/find/where/I

   Do you know _____

   _____ ?

3. the/subway/is/nearest/where/station

   Do you know _____

   _____ ?

4. what/leaves/the/time/next/train

   Could you tell me _____

   _____ ?

5. a/costs/ticket/how/much

   Could you tell me _____ ?

6. Sunday/on/is/the/if/museum/open

   Do you know _____

   _____ ?

7. to/airport/how/is/far/it/the

   Do you know _____

   _____ ?

8. phone card/I/where/can/buy/a

   Could you tell me _____

   _____ ?

2a Use the cues to rewrite the questions as indirect questions.

SURVIVE THE AMAZON

_____ 1. What should I do if a snake bites me?

(Could/tell) _____

_____

_____ 2. Do cell phones work in the Amazon?

(Do/know) _____

_____

_____ 3. How much does the ticket cost from Tokyo?

(Do/know) _____

_____

_____ 4. Where is the nearest airport?

(Could/tell) _____

_____

_____ 5. Is there a hotel in the Amazon?

(Do/know) _____

_____

_____ 6. How far is the nearest town?

(Could/tell) _____

_____

_____ 7. Can I drink the water from the river?

(Do/know) _____

_____

_____ 8. Do I need any shots before I go?

(Could/tell) _____

_____

b Match answers to the questions in Exercise 2a

SURVIVE THE AMAZON

a. It is at Belém.

b. There are many cheap hotels in and around Belém.

c. Prices vary, but usually between $2,500 and $3,000.

d. You need a shot for yellow fever.

e. Try to identify the type of snake. Tie a bandage around the bite and go to the doctor.

f. Probably not far. There are many small towns along the river.

g. Only for local calls.

h. It is safer to boil the water first.

3 Complete the conversations with the words from the box.

about	closes	what	if
Enjoy	know	sign	At
leaves	nearest	over	try

1. A: Could you tell me what time it
   _____?

   B: What, the market?

   A: Yes.

   B: _____ 6:00.

   A: 6:00. Thanks.

2. A: Excuse me. Could you tell me
   _____ we can go inside
   the palace?

   B: Yes, you can. It is $12 a ticket.

   A: OK, could we have two tickets, please?

   B: Certainly. That's $24. Thank you.
   _____ the palace.

3. A: Do you _____ if we can take
   photos of the paintings?

   B: Here in the gallery?

   A: Yes.

   B: No, you can't. There's a _____
   that says "no photography."

   A: Thanks.

4. A: Excuse me, do you know where the
   _____ subway station is?

   B: Yeah. It's _____ a five-minute
   walk from here.

   A: Thanks.

5. A: Could you tell me _____ a
   "chicken faal" is?

   B: It's a chicken dish. Very, very hot.

   A: Oh really?

   B: Very spicy. But delicious.

   A: OK, I'll _____ it.

   B: One chicken faal. Anything to drink?

6. A: Excuse me, do you know when the next
   train _____ for the airport?

   B: No, I don't know. You can ask
   _____ there.

   A: Thank you very much.

Reading

4a Read the travel article. Name two things you should **not** do in the UK.

_____

_____

Three Things You Didn't Know About the UK

Why do the English drive on the left?

In the 1700s people used their right hand to carry a sword so they rode their horses on the left-hand side of the road. But Napoleon carried his sword in his left hand and rode his horse on the right-hand side of the road. Almost everyone followed Napoleon because he ruled half the world. However, about 25 percent of countries still drive on the left, including Japan and the UK.

Top tip: Don't forget to drive on the left in the UK!

What's the difference between England and the United Kingdom?

England is one country. The United Kingdom is England, Scotland, Wales, and Northern Ireland. (The Republic of Ireland, in the south, is an independent country.) The prime minister is the head of all four of these countries.

Top tip: Never say, "You're English, aren't you?" to someone from Scotland, Ireland, or Wales.

How multicultural is the UK?

The UK is one of the world's most multicultural places. You can hear hundreds of languages in London alone. In fact, 11 percent of the UK's 62 million inhabitants were born outside the UK.

Top tip: Visit the Notting Hill carnival in late August. It is two days of multicultural music, food, and dancing.

b Mark the sentences true (*T*) or false (*F*).

_____ 1. Only the English and Japanese drive on the left.

_____ 2. England and the United Kingdom are the same place.

_____ 3. In the UK there are people from many different countries.

LESSON **1**

Vocabulary

1 Use the clues to complete the crossword puzzle.

Clues

Across

3. Doctors and lawyers earn a good _____ in my country. (Mohamed, Egypt)

5. You can learn to _____ a car when you are 17. (Mick, the UK)

7. Most women _____ children in their 20s. (Nobantu, Malawi)

8. Most people _____ when they are 65. (Dave, the US)

9. Women usually _____ married in their late 30s. (Inge, Norway)

Down

1. It's expensive to get a(n) _____ of your own. (Thais, Brazil)

2. We _____ from college in our 20s. (Laura, Canada)

4. Grandparents often _____ after the kids. (Romina, Italy)

6. Most people get _____ before they get married. (Pierre, Canada)

Grammar

2a Read what four people say about their jobs. Complete the sentences with words in the box.

Diane | don't have to   can't   have to |

1. Most people _____ afford my designs.

2. I _____ attend all the fashion shows, but I do because I enjoy them.

3. I _____ work hard before Fashion Week in October. There are many things to do.

Mike | don't have to   shouldn't   can |

4. We _____ stay out late, but some of us do after a match.

5. We _____ go to the gym, but we go sometimes.

6. You _____ earn a lot of money if you play professionally.

Rafael | can't   have to   should |

7. I _____ take long vacations because the company needs me in the office.

8. I _____ speak to all my co-workers, but I don't always have time.

9. I _____ make important business decisions.

Maria | have to   shouldn't   should |

10. I tell people that they _____ eat too much sugar.

11. I tell people that they _____ visit me two times a year.

12. I _____ look into people's mouths every day.

b Match the people from Exercise 2a with their jobs.

_____ 1. Diane   **a.** soccer player

_____ 2. Mike   **b.** dentist

_____ 3. Rafael   **c.** business person

_____ 4. Maria   **d.** fashion designer

3 Correct the sentences by crossing out one word.

1. I can't be look after the children today.
2. Do you have not to work on the weekend?
3. Should we to go to the store this morning?
4. I am have to buy a new guitar.
5. I can to swim very well.
6. You shouldn't of play there. It's dangerous.
7. Can you will help me with my bags?
8. I don't have not to do any homework tonight.

4 Circle the correct words to complete Ana's story.

Growing up in a big family

My name is Ana and I have 18 brothers and sisters. There are good and bad things about living in a big family. Money is always a problem. We *can't/don't have to* (1.) afford vacations, and we *can/have to* (2.) share bedrooms.

We are very close as a family. My parents *can't/should* (3.) look after all the children, so the older ones help the younger ones. I wash my younger brothers' clothes. Families *should/shouldn't* (4.) eat together every day, but we don't. We usually eat in two shifts (ten of us at 6:30, the rest at 7:30). We *should/have to* (5.) buy a lot of food, of course.

People ask us things like, "*should/can* (6.) you remember the names of all your brothers and sisters?" Of course I can. And they ask, "Do you buy everyone birthday presents?" The answer is no, we *don't have to/should* (7.). Birthdays *should/shouldn't* (8.) be just about presents.

5 Put the words in parentheses in order to complete the sentences.

1. A: _____ (my/in/opinion), you need a haircut.

   B: _____ (think/don't/so/I).

2. A: _____ (do/think/you/what)?

   B: You look interesting.

3. A: We need to clean this room.

   B: _____ (right/you're/probably).

4. A: Beautiful scenery. _____ (think/you/so/don't)?

   B: _____ (not/sure/so/I'm).

Reading

1 Read the article. Then answer the questions. Write *C* (Carnegie), *S* (Soros), *CS* (both of them), or *N* (neither of them).

Friends of the World

Andrew Carnegie

Andrew Carnegie was born in Scotland in 1835. His family was very poor. When Carnegie was 13 years old, the family moved to Pittsburgh in the US. He didn't finish his education, but a rich man named James Anderson gave Carnegie books from his library.

As a young man, Carnegie worked on the railway. He invested his money in business and made money quickly. In 1873 he started his own steel company. By 1900, the company was producing 25 percent of the steel in the US.

There were no free public libraries in the US, so Carnegie built 2,800 of them. He also gave a lot of money to charity.

Finally he returned to Scotland, where he wrote several books. He gave away 90 percent of his money and died in 1919.

George Soros

George Soros was born in Budapest, Hungary, in 1930. An intelligent young man, Soros went to England in 1947 and studied at the London School of Economics. Nine years later, he went to the US. Soros started an international investment company and became rich quickly. He understood international financial markets and was called "the man who broke the Bank of England" when, in 1992, he earned $1.1 billion in one day.

Soros created institutions to solve world problems in health, education, the media, and human rights. These institutions spend $400 million a year. Soros now writes books about politics, economics, and society.

_____ **1.** Who left his country when he was a teenager?

_____ **2.** Who had a good education?

_____ **3.** Which of them made his money in the US?

_____ **4.** Which of them became a politician?

_____ **5.** Who created new institutions to help people?

_____ **6.** Who gave money to improve education?

_____ **7.** Who returned to his home country to live?

_____ **8.** Who wrote books?

2 Find the words in the article. Match the definitions to the words.

_____ **1.** invest in

_____ **2.** charity

_____ **3.** institution

_____ **4.** human rights

a. a big organization

b. put money into a business

c. an organization that gives money or things to people who need help

d. things that everyone should be free to do or have

Grammar

3 Cross out the incorrect choice.

1. I haven't been to a movie *in years/since June/since years*.

2. We haven't played tennis *since last year/ages ago/for months*.

3. She's worked here *for two weeks/since three months/for a long time*.

4. I've played the piano *since I was a child/since ages/for five years*.

5. Have you lived here *for a long time/since January/years ago*?

6. Has she known him *for years/since last July/for February*?

7. I haven't seen you *since I was in Mexico/for a year or two/since months*.

8. He's been on the team *since two weeks/since he scored his first goal/for too long*.

4 Use the cues to complete sentences with the same meaning.

1. I arrived in China last Thursday.
   (here) I've been _____ Thursday.

2. It is 2012. She moved here in 2007.
   (lived) She _____ five years.

3. I met John at school. He's my best friend.
   (known) I've _____ we were at school.

4. Letitia doesn't smoke. She stopped years ago.
   (hasn't) Letitia _____ years.

5. I last saw Giorgio seven days ago.
   (haven't) I _____ last week.

6. I first played tennis in 1990, and I still play.
   (have) I _____ 1990.

7. We arrived at 6:00 A.M., and it's now 9:00 A.M.!
   (been) We _____ three hours!

5 Complete the conversations. Use the present perfect form of the verbs in parentheses.

1. A: How long _____ (they/live) here?
   B: Twenty-four hours!

2. A: When did he arrive?
   B: _____ (he/be) here all evening.

3. A: Where are the dogs?
   B: I don't know. _____
      (I/not see) them for ages.

4. A: How long _____ (you/know) him?
   B: Ten years.

5. A: Nice hairstyle!
   B: _____ (she/have) it for years.

6. A: Is Greg coming?
   B: I don't know. _____
      (we/not speak) to him for weeks.

Vocabulary

6 Choose the correct word or words to complete the email.

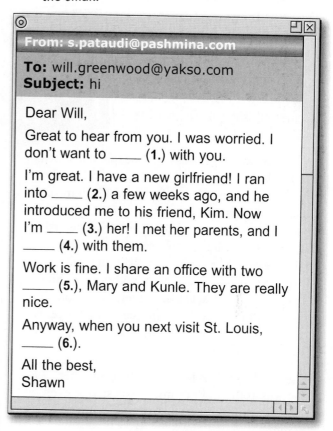

From: s.pataudi@pashmina.com

To: will.greenwood@yakso.com
Subject: hi

Dear Will,

Great to hear from you. I was worried. I don't want to _____ (**1.**) with you.

I'm great. I have a new girlfriend! I ran into _____ (**2.**) a few weeks ago, and he introduced me to his friend, Kim. Now I'm _____ (**3.**) her! I met her parents, and I _____ (**4.**) with them.

Work is fine. I share an office with two _____ (**5.**), Mary and Kunle. They are really nice.

Anyway, when you next visit St. Louis, _____ (**6.**).

All the best,
Shawn

1. **a.** lose touch   **b.** miss touch   **c.** stop touch
2. **a.** best friends   **b.** an old friend   **c.** a girlfriend
3. **a.** going on   **b.** going out   **c.** going out with
4 **a.** got along well   **b.** got in   **c.** got over
5. **a.** work people   **b.** work friends   **c.** co-workers
6. **a.** get on touch   **b.** come in touch   **c.** get in touch

Writing

7 Add punctuation and capital letters to the story.

since college ive worked as a sales representative
for a publishing company its a nice job my
colleagues are really friendly and i travel a lot these
days im living in Mazatlan i've been here two years,
and i love the city id love to hear from you
julia mendez

Reading

1a Read the story and circle the best title.
  a. Ten Ways to Live Happily
  b. A Long, Long Life
  c. Jean Calment's Lawyer

Jeanne Calment was born in 1875 and died in 1997. At 122 years old, she was the world's oldest person.

She was born in Arles and became a celebrity in her home town. Journalists asked her about the secrets of her **long life**. She told them she used to eat chocolate, put olive oil on her skin, **smoke two cigarettes a day**, and **drink red wine**. But the truth, her doctor said, is that she never **felt stressed**. She once said, "If you can't do anything about it, why worry about it?" She also had a good **sense of humor**. When one visitor said to her, "Maybe see you next year," she replied, "I don't see why not. You don't look so bad to me."

She used to **ride a bike** (she stopped when she was 100), and her mind was strong even after her body **grew old**. She said, "I never **get bored**."

The best **true Calment story** was about her house. When she was 90, her lawyer bought the house. He paid her only $400 a month, a very small **amount of money**. His plan was to get the house when Jeanne Calment died. But he died first, at the age of 77, after paying $180,000, much more than the house was worth!

b Cover the story in Exercise 1a. Then match the words to make phrases from the story.

_____ 1. amount	a. cigarettes
_____ 2. true	b. humor
_____ 3. smoke	c. of money
_____ 4. drink	d. old
_____ 5. feel	e. a bike
_____ 6. sense of	f. wine
_____ 7. ride	g. life
_____ 8. grow	h. stressed
_____ 9. get	i. bored
_____ 10. long	j. story

c Use the phrases in Exercise 1b to complete the summary. You may need to change the verb form.

1. She is famous because she lived a(n) _____ _____.
2. She never _____ _____.
3. She had a good _____ _____ _____.
4. She _____ _____ _____ until she was 100.
5. Her mind stayed young even when her body _____ _____.
6. There is a funny _____ _____ about her house and her lawyer.
7. Her lawyer thought he would pay her a small _____ _____ _____ for the house. He was wrong!

Grammar

2a Write *Yes/No* questions using *used to* and the cues.

Ex: play/any instruments
Did you use to play any instruments?

1. watch/a lot of TV _____
   _____
2. go abroad/for vacation _____
   _____
3. cook/for your parents _____
   _____
4. help your mother/around the house _____
   _____
5. get/a lot of exercise _____
   _____

b Match the answers to the questions in Exercise 2a.
  a. Yes. I always washed the dishes.
  b. No, I hated sports.
  c. Yes. I went to Jamaica, Mexico, . . .
  d. No. My father used to make the dinner.
  e. Yes, four hours every day.

Communication

3a Look at the picture and complete the sentences.

Main Street Today

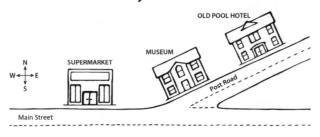

A: This town has changed a lot. You see the supermarket on the left here?

B: Yes.

A: That _____ (1.) a school.

B: Really?

A: Yes, it was my school. But about ten years ago they closed it. Now it's a supermarket.

B: I see.

A: On the south side of the street, you see the _____ (2.)?

B: Yes.

A: There _____ (3.) a sports field there. We played soccer there every day.

B: A sports field?

A: That's right.

B: Where are we now?

A: This is Post Road. The museum _____ (4.) a hospital.

B: Really?

A: Yes. They built the museum about ten years ago.

B: What type of _____ (5.) is it?

A: Art. It has a lot of old art.

B: Old Pool Hotel. Didn't there _____ (6.) a swimming pool here?

A: Yes. There weren't any tourists in the past.

B: Did you swim there when you were young?

A: No, I _____ (7.) swim there. I preferred the beach.

b Read the conversation again and complete the chart.

Is now	Used to be
A. supermarket	
B. parking lot	
C. museum	
D. Old Pool Hotel	

Vocabulary

4 Use the clues to complete the puzzle. What is the hidden word?

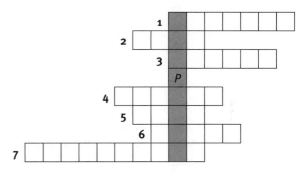

Clues

1. A: Do you always eat good food, like fruit and vegetables?
   B: Yes. I like to eat h_____ food.

2. A: Do you always eat hamburgers and chocolate?
   B: Yes. I love eating junk f_____!

3. A: Did you use to smoke?
   B: Yes. I used to be a _____r.

4. A: Do you like reading, playing chess, and doing crosswords?
   B: Yes. I like to be mentally a_____.

5. A: Do you always go to bed at 3 A.M.?
   B: Yes. I go to bed very l_____.

6. A: Do you always carry bottles in your bag?
   B: Yes. I drink a lot of w_____.

7. A: Do you always feel good about life?
   B: Yes. I always think p_____y.

LESSON 1

Vocabulary

1 Use the clues to complete the crossword puzzle.

Clues

Down

1. Quebec, Ontario, and British Columbia are all provinces of _____.
2. This South American country is known for the spring celebration *Carnaval*.
4. Actress Nicole Kidman is this nationality.
6. Which continent is home to Italy?
7. With 1.3 billion people, this is the most populated country in the world.

Across

3. This is the nationality of people who live in the United States.
5. In which Asian country is Mount Fuji situated?
8. The Black Forest is in which country?
9. What nationality was the painter Pablo Picasso?

2 Use the words in the box to complete the sentences.

> mountain   island   river   forest   sea
> beaches   ocean   lake   desert

1. Australia is the biggest _____ in the world.
2. The Pacific is the largest _____ in the world.
3. The Nile is the longest _____ in the world.
4. The highest _____ in the Alps is Mont Blanc.
5. The mountains of Canada are covered in a thick _____.
6. The long, white _____ in Brazil are beautiful.
7. About 30% of the country of Mexico is a(n) _____.
8. The Caspian _____ is surrounded by land so it is, in fact, the world's biggest _____.

Grammar

3 Complete the conversations using *will* or *won't* and a verb from the box.

> know   be   pay   carry   sleep   show

1. A: Could we talk about this tomorrow?
   B: No. I _____ here tomorrow.
2. A: I don't have any money for the taxi.
   B: It's OK. I _____ for it.
3. A: Would you like some coffee?
   B: No, thanks. I _____ tonight if I drink it now.
4. A: How does this computer work?
   B: Come here and I _____ you.
5. A: How did you do on the test?
   B: I _____ until I go back to school.
6. A: This bag is very heavy!
   B: Let me help. I _____ it for you.

4 Circle the correct words.

1. I'm going out to lunch. _I see you/I'll see you_ later.
2. The weather is getting better. I think _I'll go/ I go_ to the beach this weekend.
3. _Will you stay/Do you stay_ in the same hotel when you come back next month?
4. I'm very tired. _I'll finish/I finish_ this report tomorrow.
5. Is that the phone ringing? _I'll get/I get_ it.
6. I love soccer. _I play/I'll play_ every weekend.
7. My mother is in the hospital, so _I visit/I'll visit_ her every day.
8. I haven't spoken to Jenny for ages. _I send/ I'll send_ her a postcard.

Reading

5a You are going to read about two tourist destinations: Mexico and Western Australia. Before you read, guess the answers to the questions. Write _M_ (Mexico), _WA_ (Western Australia), or _B_ (both).

Where . . .

_____ 1. do people speak different languages in the different areas?

_____ 2. can you explore the desert?

_____ 3. can you find beautiful beaches?

_____ 4. can you visit lakes in the mountains?

_____ 5. can you swim with dolphins?

b Read the articles to check your answers.

MEXICO is <u>one of North America's most</u>[1] beautiful countries. Cities like Mexico City seem like a concrete jungle, and then you look up and see the wonderful peaks of Iztaccíhuatl. <u>In the south,</u>[2] the landscape has natural beauty, with cool mountain lakes, hot deserts, and miles and miles of beaches. Each of Mexico's cities has a different character, from the exciting energy of Guadalajara to the relaxing streets of Guanajuato. Mexican people <u>are famous for</u>[3] their warmth and hospitality, so traveling around the country is easy. Most people speak Spanish, but some Mexicans also speak other languages such as Nahuatl. Mexico's historic cities and beautiful beaches <u>attract visitors throughout the year.</u>[4]

Western Australia

Sun, adventure, a beautiful environment, and friendly people. This is what you'll find on a vacation to Western Australia.

Western Australia has a natural beauty, long days of sunshine, clear blue skies, and great beaches. <u>Come to Western Australia to</u>[5] swim with wild dolphins, walk through the ancient forest, or sleep under the stars in the Outback desert. <u>Why not start your vacation</u>[6] in the capital city of Western Australia, Perth? You can spend an afternoon sitting outside a pub and enjoying a cool drink with the locals.

6 Mark these sentences true (_T_), false (_F_), or no information (_NI_).

Mexico

_____ 1. Guadalajara is more beautiful than Guanajuato.

_____ 2. The main language in Mexico is Mexican.

_____ 3. It's difficult to travel from one city to another city.

Western Australia

_____ 4. _Outback_ is a town.

_____ 5. Perth is the capital of Western Australia.

_____ 6. There are a lot of pubs.

7 Match each underlined phrase in the article to a similar phrase below.

_____ a. It's a good idea to start your vacation . . .

_____ b. well-known because of

_____ c. In the south/east/west . . .

_____ d. Visit . . . in order to . . .

_____ e. There are some very famous/ beautiful/expensive places. This is one of them.

_____ f. tourists like to visit this place all year

Grammar

1 Look at the pictures. Complete the sentences using *too* or *enough* and words from the box.

> suitcases   crowded   loud   money   small   tall

1. The music is _____
_____.

2. He isn't _____
_____.

3. They have _____
many _____.

4. He doesn't have
_____
_____ to buy food.

5. His jacket is _____
_____ for him.

6. The train is
_____
_____.

2 Complete the sentences using *too, too much, too many,* or *enough.*

1. It's _____ crowded for me in the city. I prefer the country.

2. There are _____ people on the beach today.

3. There aren't _____ buses. We always have to wait.

4. There's _____ noise in here. I'm going to work next door.

5. It's _____ hot in the office. Can you turn on the air-conditioning?

6. I didn't have _____ money to buy the guitar.

7. I have _____ homework to do. I'll never finish by tomorrow!

3 Complete the sentences using *too, too much, too many,* or *enough,* and the cues.

1. I'm not going to play soccer tonight. I'm _____ (tired).

2. You're not working _____ (hard). You won't pass your test.

3. He spends _____ (time) on the computer. He never goes out.

4. We would like to buy a new car, but it's _____ (expensive).

5. Those children eat _____ (hamburgers). It's not good for them.

6. We didn't go into the museum because there were _____ (people).

7. You can't come into this club. You are not _____ (old).

Vocabulary

4 Use the pictures to complete the sentences.

1. I need to clean my house, but my _____ isn't working.

2. Come and listen to my music. I've got a new _____.

3. Your hair is still wet. Do you want to use my _____?

4. You don't need to wash the dishes. We have a _____.

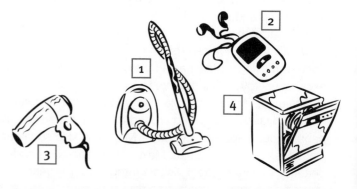

Communication

5a Complete the conversation about a TV show, using the words from the box.

> TV   show   teenagers   cell phones   interesting   parking lots   confusing   technology

A: Have you seen that TV show *Amish in the City*?

B: No. Why?

A: Oh. It's really _____ (1.). It's about five Amish people. The Amish live in religious communities in the US countryside, and they don't have _____ (2.).

B: No technology? Don't they have computers?

A: No. Nothing. They build their own houses and ride horses. They don't have cars or _____ (3.) or anything.

B: Wow. So what happens in the _____ (4.)?

A: Well, it takes five Amish teenagers to live in a big house in Los Angeles, with some other _____ (5.), who are not Amish.

B: So the Los Angeles kids teach these Amish people about the modern world?

A: Yes. That's right. The Amish have never watched _____ (6.) before, or seen MP3 players, videos, dishwashers. Nothing!

B: They've never seen them?

A: No. And they go to the beach, and the Amish have never seen the ocean before. It's really good.

B: Yes, it sounds interesting.

A: They go out to discos, and go shopping.

B: And do the Amish like what they see? Do they like the modern world?

A: Well, they find it very _____ (7.). They don't know what to think. The girls like wearing the new clothes. And everything is very interesting for them, even things like _____ (8.)!

Amish in the City

b Read the conversation again. Then circle the best description.

1. *Amish in the City* takes five teenagers from an Amish community, who know nothing about technology, and moves them to live with other teenagers in Los Angeles. They are going to learn about modern life in Los Angeles.

2. *Amish in the City* takes five Los Angeles teenagers to a community of Amish people, where they learn how to live without modern technology. There are no cars, no cell phones, and no TV.

6 Circle the correct words.

1. I think we *should/would* take the digital camera *because/so* it's better.

2. I *like/'d like* to take the MP3 player. I *couldn't/mustn't* live without it!

3. We'd like *choose/to choose* Bogotá for the new office. The *main/mains* reason is that it is a busy city.

4. I think we should *take/to take* a taxi to the airport. I'm *so/too* lazy to carry these bags on the train.

5. We think we should *go/to go* to the hotel first *because/because of* the restaurant is a long way from here.

Grammar

1   Circle the correct words.

1. **A:** _Do you like/Would you like_ a glass of water?

    B: Yes, please.

2. **A:** _Do you like/Would you like_ chocolate?

    B: Yes, I eat it every day.

3. **A:** Are you free this afternoon? Nadia _would like/likes_ to meet you for coffee.

    B: Yes. Tell her I can meet her at 4 P.M.

4. **A:** What time _do you like/would you like_ to leave?

    B: Let's leave at 6:30 P.M.

5. **A:** _Do you like/Would you like_ going out at night?

    B: Yes, but I don't stay out late.

6. **A:** Do you have Phil's email address? _I like/I'd like_ to write to him, but I don't have his address here.

    B: Yes. It's philip.denton@aoi.com

2a   Complete the paragraph, using words from the box.

> look like   am I like   likes   like
>
> don't like   's he like   'd like

   My brother and I are twins, but we're very different. We don't _____ (1.) each other, because Marc has dark hair, and I have blond hair. We _____ (2.) the same things, either. We eat different kinds of food, see different friends, and have different interests. He _____ (3.) playing soccer, but I like reading books. I _____ (4.) going out to parties, but he likes to stay at home and watch sports on TV. What _____ (5.)? Well, he's great at sports, but he's not very friendly. And what _____ (6.)? I have lots of friends, but I am terrible at sports! I _____ (7.) to be better at sports, but I think it's too late now. I'm nearly 40!

b   Look at the pictures. Which man wrote the paragraph in Exercise 2a? _____ Which man is Marc? _____

3   Circle the correct word or phrase to complete each sentence.

1. Your eyes _look like/like/would like_ Amanda's. Are you two sisters?

2. Do you _would like/like/are like_ living in China?

3. _Would you like/Do you like/Are you like_ to come to lunch with us?

4. **A:** I painted my new apartment yesterday.

    B: Really? What _would you/does it look/do you look_ like?

5. **A:** I prefer the old part of the city.

    B: Why? What _would you/is it look/is it_ like?

6. **A:** _Would you/Do you/Are you_ like a drink?

    B: Thank you. I _like/'d like/look like_ an orange juice.

7. **A:** I don't know Mario. What _does he look/is he look/would he_ like?

    B: He's tall, with dark hair and blue eyes.

8. **A:** _Would you like/Do you like/Are you like_ cooking?

    B: Yes. I love it.

9. **A:** What _is/does/looks_ your new teacher like?

    B: She's really good. I like her.

10. **A:** You've been to Brazil. _What do you/What's it/What would you_ like?

    B: It's very beautiful, and the people are very friendly.

Reading

4 Read the story. Then correct the sentences about the story.

The Richest Man in the World by Carlos Blanco

1 He sat in his yard, drinking coffee. On the sofa behind him there was a dishwasher and a vacuum cleaner. Next to the sofa there was a stove with a hairdryer. And as the sun got higher and hotter, he just sat there on his chair drinking coffee.

5 It was Sunday, and there were families walking back from church. One old couple saw him and stopped.

"Hello there!" said the old man.

"Good morning," said the man on the chair.

10 The old couple stood there.

"Mister," said the old man. "We see you have a dishwasher."

"That's right," said the man drinking coffee.

"Is it for sale? I mean, do you want to sell <u>it</u>?"

15 "For sale? I wouldn't say that exactly."

"Because we would like to buy it, you see."

"OK," said the man. "How much do you want to pay?"

The old man said, "I only have ten dollars on me."

20 "Ten dollars?"

The old man put his hand in his pocket and pulled out some coins, some paper, a bag of tobacco.

"I know <u>it</u>'s not enough, but I can get more. I can go home and get you more money, or we can wait till

25 tomorrow when the bank is open."

"Ten dollars?" said the man drinking coffee. He put the cup down. "Ten dollars is too much. I'll sell it to you for two fifty."

The old couple looked at each other. And they

30 bought the dishwasher for two dollars and fifty cents, and they called their sons, who lived with them, and the sons carried it away.

A little later, a young family came by. They

looked at the man, and the man looked at them: five

35 children, no shoes, one dog on a string.

"What's your dog's name?" said the man.

The youngest boy shouted, "Loopy! <u>His</u> name's Loopy!"

The boy dropped the string and Loopy walked

40 across the yard, his nose to the ground. He came to the sofa and smelled the ghosts of other dogs.

"Hey, Mister," said the young woman. "Are you selling that stove?"

"Yes, I am. But it'll cost you."

45 "How much?"

"Two dollars. And if that's too much, I'll take one fifty."

And the mother bought the stove for one dollar and twelve cents, and the children picked <u>it</u> up and

50 carried it home, all except the youngest boy who ran with the dog on a string.

A little later, the man sold his vacuum cleaner to a young couple for ten cents. Then he sold his hairdryer to an old lady with blue hair. Then finally he even

55 sold the sofa. Now, in the early evening, there was nothing in his yard except the last heat of the sun and a small breath of wind in the man's face.

The boy with the dog on a string came back.

"Hello, Loopy!" said the man.

60 "Can I ask you something, Mister?"

"Of course you can."

"Mister, are you rich?"

The man smiled. He looked at the first stars shining and a big lemon moon behind a tree. He had

65 eight dollars and seventy cents in his hand.

"Yes," he said. "I'm the richest man in the world."

1. A man was drinking coffee in his house.
2. A young couple walked past and asked if they could buy his dishwasher.
3. The old man only had $5.
4. They bought the dishwasher for $2.15.
5. At the end of the day, he had $870.
6. When the young boy returned with his dog, the old man told him that he was the happiest man in the world.

Writing

5 Find these <u>underlined</u> words in the story in Exercise 4. What do they refer to?

1. it (*line 14*) _____
2. it (*line 23*) _____
3. his (*line 37*) _____
4. it (*line 49*) _____

6 Why do you think the man was the richest man in the world?

_____

_____

_____

_____

_____

Comparatives and superlatives

1 Complete the sentences using the adjectives in parentheses. Use a comparative or superlative.

1. Kenya is _____ (hot) than Canada.
2. Wolves are _____ (dangerous) than dogs.
3. Elephants are _____ (large) land mammals in the world.
4. Russ is _____ (young) than me.
5. The psychology course is _____ (interesting) than the history course.
6. *Casablanca* is _____ (romantic) movie I've ever seen.
7. The Monte Desert is _____ (small) than the Sahara.
8. That was _____ (good) day of my life.
9. Sarah is _____ (lazy) than her sister.
10. Hannah bought _____ (pretty) dress in the store.

Indirect questions

2 Make the questions indirect.

Ex: When does the library open?
Could you tell me _when the library opens_ ?

1. (What time does the bus leave?) Could you tell me _____ ?
2. (How much do these shoes cost?) Could you tell me _____ ?
3. (How does this photocopier work?) Could you tell me _____ ?
4. (What is the capital of Mexico?) Do you know _____ ?
5. (When does the next train leave?) Do you know _____ ?
6. (Is the museum open on Sundays?) Could you tell me _____ ?
7. (Is there a train to Cartagena?) Do you know _____ ?

should, can, have to

3 Use the cues to make sentences with the same meaning.

1. It's a good idea to buy our tickets early.
   (should) We _____ our tickets early.
2. It isn't necessary to pay for children.
   (have) You _____ pay for children.
3. She needs to take her test again.
   (has) She _____ her test again.
4. Is it possible for me to go home now?
   (Can) _____ home now?
5. It's not a good idea to arrive late.
   (shouldn't) We _____ late.
6. Is it necessary to read this book?
   (have) Do we _____ this book?
7. It's healthy to eat more vegetables.
   (should) You _____ more vegetables.
8. Is it necessary for me to leave?
   (have) Do _____ leave?

Used to and present perfect with *for* and *since*

4 Complete the clauses with *used to* and the words in parentheses. Then match them with the clauses below to form sentences. Circle *for* or *since*.

_____ 1. I _____ (smoke),
_____ 2. She _____ (be) good at the guitar,
_____ 3. We _____ (not/like) each other when we were children,
_____ 4. Mom and Dad _____ (travel) a lot,
_____ 5. I _____ (not/cook) much pasta,

a. but we've been friends _for/since_ the last few months.
b. but I've eaten a lot of it _for/since_ I went to Italy.
c. but I haven't had a cigarette _for/since_ last year.
d. but they haven't had a vacation _for/since_ 2007.
e. but she hasn't played _for/since_ two years.

Will with adverbs

5 Make predictions using *will/won't* and the words in parentheses. Then circle the correct word.

1. Where _____ (you/have) breakfast? Jojo's Café serves *very/enough* good food.

2. She _____ (stay) in this hotel because it's *too/enough* expensive.

3. What time _____ (they/arrive)? Not *enough/very* late, I hope.

4. My new apartment is *too/very* close to my office, so I _____ (need) to drive to work.

5. She _____ (study) law if her test results are good *very/enough*.

6. It's *too/enough* cold to eat outside. Also, I think it _____ (rain) this afternoon.

7. It's a *very/too* short movie, so we _____ (be) home late.

8. Where _____ (you/go) on your next vacation? Bali is beautiful and not *very/ enough* expensive.

9. We _____ (go) swimming this afternoon because the water is *enough/ too* cold.

Uses of *like*

6 Put the words in order to make questions.

1. you/Would/like/coffee

   _____ ?

2. she/her/sister/look/Does/like

   _____ ?

3. do/in/free/What/you/doing/like/time/your

   _____ ?

4. is/John's/like/What/girlfriend

   _____ ?

5. would/go/to/Where/you/like/tomorrow

   _____ ?

6. you/like/Who/look/do

   _____ ?

7. book/like/is/What/that

   _____ ?

Vocabulary

7 Read the definitions and write words from Units 4, 5, and 6. Hint: The words are in alphabetical order!

1. _____ (*adj*): doesn't fear anything (Unit 4 Lesson 1)

2. _____ (*n*): something that is difficult to do (Unit 4, Warm Up)

3. _____ (*n*): place with a lot of sand and not much water (Unit 6 Lesson 1)

4. _____ (*n*): geographical feature with many big trees (Unit 6 Lesson 1)

5. _____ (*adj*): giving (Unit 4 Lesson 1)

6. _____ (*adv*): good for you (Unit 5 Lesson 3)

7. _____ (*adj*): not stupid (Unit 4 Lesson 1)

8. _____ (*adj*): . . . food – what you eat in fast food restaurants (Unit 5 Lesson 3)

9. _____ (*v*): . . . touch – not stay in contact (Unit 5 Lesson 2)

10. _____ (*n*): small machine for listening to music and watching videos (Unit 6 Lesson 2)

11. _____ (*n*): very big body of water (Unit 6 Lesson 1)

12. _____ (*v*): when an older person stops working (Unit 5, Warm Up)

13. _____ (*n*): a person who smokes (Unit 5 Lesson 3)

14. _____ (*adj*): has a lot of natural ability (Unit 4 Lesson 1)

English in Common ActiveBook
Installation Instructions

Windows
- Insert the disc into the CD-ROM drive of your computer. On most computers, the program will begin automatically.
- If the program does not begin automatically, open "My Computer."
- Right-click on the CD-ROM icon. Click on Open.

Macintosh
- Insert the disc into the CD-ROM drive of your computer.
- Double-click on the CD-ROM icon on your desktop.
- Double click on the "START_OSX" file to run the program. Leave the CD-ROM in the computer while using the program.

Note: You must have administrator privileges on the computer to install the program. To install:
- **Windows:** Double-click on the "install" file to start the installation.
- **Macintosh:** Copy all files from the CD-ROM to a folder on your hard drive.

ActiveBook System Requirements

	PC Compatible	Macintosh Compatible
Operating System	Microsoft Windows® XP, Vista, Windows 7	Mac OSX v. (10.4 & 10.5)
Processor	Intel Pentium® IV 1000MHz or faster processor (or equivalent)	PowerPC & Intel processor 500MHz or faster processor (or equivalent)
RAM	512 MB RAM minimum or higher	512 MB RAM minimum or higher
Internet Browser	Microsoft Internet Explorer® 7.x or Mozilla Firefox™ 4.x, or higher	Safari® 3.x, Mozilla Firefox™ 4.x, or higher
Plug-ins	Adobe PDF 8, Adobe Flash 9, or higher	Adobe PDF 8, Adobe Flash 9, or higher
Hardware	Computer CD-ROM drive, sound card and speakers or headphones	Computer CD-ROM drive, sound card and speakers or headphones
Monitor Resolution	1024x768	1024x768
Internet Connection	DSL, cable/broadband, T1, or other high-speed connection required to download plug-ins	

TECHNICAL SUPPORT

For Technical Product Support, please visit our support website at www.PearsonLongmanSupport.com. You can search our *Knowledgebase* for frequently asked questions, instantly *Chat* with an available support representative, or *Submit a Ticket/Request* for assistance.